CW00516982

High Fiber Cookbook

Preparing and cooking with High Fiber Ingredients: Directions and Nutrition (per serve) (More than 300 dishes)

Patricia J. Leffel

Table of Content

Introduction:

Our High Fiber Cookbook welcomes you to a world of excellent health and tasty food. In this vast collection, we look at the excellent health benefits and delicious tastes of foods high in fibre. Fibre isn't just an essential part of a healthy diet; it's also a way to improve your health by helping your digestive system, heart health, weight control, and blood sugar levels.

Our cookbook is designed to help you learn about a wide range of high-fibre foods, from the common to the unusual. This cookbook is meant to excite, teach, and please your taste buds, no matter how long you've been interested in health or how soon you've started a fibre-rich diet.

If you look through the pages of this cookbook, you'll find an incredible trove of recipes that show how nutrition and taste can go together. Our cookbook has recipes for everything, from breakfasts that give you the energy to start the day to lunches and dinners that are as healthy as they are tasty. Fibre is the show's star in creative salads, soul-warming soups, filling grain bowls, and delicious main dishes.

We know that eating for health shouldn't mean giving up on taste, so our recipes balance healthy ingredients and delicious flavours. Our recipe has something for everyone, whether you want more fibre, control your weight, or eat delicious food.

Each recipe comes with easy-to-follow steps, information about how healthy it is, and ways to add more fibre to your daily life. With this cookbook as your guide, you will not only learn new ways to cook, but you will also start living a better life.

So, if you want to change your diet, try new foods, or get creative in the kitchen, the High Fiber Cookbook is here to help you. Get ready to enjoy the benefits of fibre one delicious dish at a time and feel good about giving your body and taste buds what they need.

HEARTY LENTIL AND VEGETABLE SOUP

Nutrition (per serving):

- Calories: 180
- Protein: 10g
- Carbohydrates: 30g
- Fiber: 12g
- Fat: 2g

Ingredients:

- 1 cup dried green or brown lentils, rinsed and drained
- 1 onion, chopped
- 2 carrots, peeled and diced
- 2 celery stalks, diced
- 3 garlic cloves, minced
- 1 can (14 oz) diced tomatoes
- 6 cups vegetable broth
- 1 teaspoon ground cumin
- 1 teaspoon smoked paprika
- Salt and pepper to taste
- 2 cups chopped spinach or kale

Instructions:

1. Cook the onion, carrots, and celery in a big pot over medium heat until soft.
2. Add the garlic that has been chopped, cumin, and smoked paprika. Keep cooking for one more minute.
3. Put the lentils, diced tomatoes, and veggie broth in the pot. Get it to boil.
4. Turn down the heat, cover, and let the lentils simmer for about 25 to 30 minutes or until soft.
5. Salt and pepper can be added to taste. Stir in the chopped spinach or kale and cook until it wilts.

6. Serve the soup warm. You can also put fresh herbs on top if you want.

FIBER-PACKED BREAKFAST PARFAIT

Nutrition (per serving):

- Calories: 280
- Protein: 12g
- Carbohydrates: 45g
- Fiber: 10g
- Fat: 7g

Ingredients:

- 1 cup Greek yogurt
- 1/2 cup mixed berries (such as strawberries, blueberries, and raspberries)
- 1/4 cup granola (with at least 5g of fibre per serving)
- 2 tablespoons chia seeds
- 1 tablespoon honey or maple syrup
- 1 teaspoon vanilla extract

Instructions:

1. Start by putting 1/4 cup of Greek yoghurt in the bottom of a bowl or glass.
2. Mix some berries and put them on top of the yoghurt.
3. Sprinkle the berries with 1 tablespoon of chia seeds.
4. Drizzle the chia seeds with 1/2 tablespoon of honey or maple syrup.
5. As the next layer, add another 1/4 cup of Greek yoghurt.

6. On top of the yoghurt, sprinkle some granola.
7. Add the vanilla extract and the rest of the honey or maple syrup to the yoghurt.
8. Add another layer of mixed berries on top to finish.
9. Serve immediately or put in the fridge until you're ready to eat.

QUINOA-STUFFED BELL PEPPERS

Nutrition (per serving, based on one stuffed pepper):

- Calories: 320
- Protein: 12g
- Carbohydrates: 50g
- Fiber: 8g
- Fat: 9g

Ingredients:

- 4 large bell peppers, any colour
- 1 cup quinoa, rinsed and drained
- 2 cups vegetable broth
- 1 can (14 oz) black beans, drained and rinsed
- 1 cup corn kernels (fresh, frozen, or canned)
- 1 teaspoon ground cumin
- 1/2 teaspoon chilli powder
- Salt and pepper to taste
- 1 cup shredded cheddar cheese (optional)

Instructions:

1. Turn the oven on and set it to 375°F (190°C).

2. Remove the seeds and skins from the bell peppers and cut off the tops.
3. Bring the vegetable soup to a boil in a pot. Add the quinoa, turn the heat down to low, cover, and cook for about 15 minutes until the quinoa is cooked and the liquid is absorbed.
4. Mix the cooked quinoa, black beans, corn, cumin powder, chilli powder, salt, and pepper in a bowl.
5. Stuff the rice mix into each bell pepper.
6. Put the peppers in an oven dish and cover them with aluminium foil.
7. Bake the peppers for about 25 to 30 minutes or until soft.
8. If you want to use cheese, take off the paper and sprinkle the peppers with shredded cheddar cheese. Bake for another 5 minutes or until the cheese is melted.
9. Serve the peppers with the stuffing hot.

CREAMY CHICKPEA AND SPINACH CURRY

Nutrition (per serving):

- Calories: 280
- Protein: 10g
- Carbohydrates: 40g
- Fiber: 10g
- Fat: 10g

Ingredients:

- 2 cans (15 oz each) chickpeas, drained and rinsed
- 1 onion, chopped

- 2 cloves garlic, minced
- 1 tablespoon curry powder
- 1 teaspoon ground cumin
- 1/2 teaspoon ground turmeric
- 1/2 teaspoon ground ginger
- 1/4 teaspoon cayenne pepper (adjust to taste)
- 1 can (14 oz) diced tomatoes
- 1 can (14 oz) coconut milk
- 4 cups fresh spinach leaves
- Salt and pepper to taste
- Fresh cilantro, chopped (for garnish)
- Cooked brown rice (for serving)

Instructions:

1. In a big pan, cook the chopped onion until it turns transparent.
2. Add the chopped garlic, curry powder, cumin powder, turmeric powder, ginger powder, and cayenne pepper. Cook for about a minute or until the smell is pleasant.
3. Put the chickpeas, diced tomatoes with their juices, and coconut milk in the pan. Mix well to blend.
4. Bring the mixture to a boil and cook for 10–15 minutes to let the flavours blend.
5. Stir in the fresh spinach and cook until it wilts.
6. Salt and pepper the curry to your taste.
7. The chickpea and spinach soup should be served over cooked brown rice.
8. Before serving, sprinkle chopped cilantro on top.

WHOLE WHEAT BANANA NUT MUFFINS

Nutrition (per muffin):

- Calories: 180
- Protein: 6g
- Carbohydrates: 30g
- Fiber: 5g
- Fat: 6g

Ingredients:

- 2 ripe bananas, mashed
- 1/4 cup honey or maple syrup
- 1/4 cup Greek yogurt
- 1/4 cup unsweetened applesauce
- 1 egg
- 1 teaspoon vanilla extract
- 1 cup whole wheat flour
- 1/2 cup rolled oats
- 1 teaspoon baking powder
- 1/2 teaspoon baking soda
- 1/2 teaspoon cinnamon
- 1/4 teaspoon salt
- 1/2 cup chopped walnuts or pecans

Instructions:

1. Turn the oven on and set it to 350°F (175°C). Put paper plates in a muffin tin or grease the cups.
2. Mix the mashed bananas, honey or maple syrup, Greek yoghurt, applesauce, egg, and vanilla extract in a bowl. Blend well.

3. Mix the whole wheat flour, rolled oats, baking powder, baking soda, cinnamon, and salt in another bowl.
4. Mix the wet and dry ingredients until they are just mixed. Refrain from mixing too much.
5. Mix in the chopped pecans or walnuts.
6. Fill each muffin cup about two-thirds of the way with the batter.
7. Bake for 18–20 minutes, or until a toothpick put into the middle of a muffin comes out clean.
8. Let the muffins cool for a few minutes in the pan before moving them to a wire rack to finish cooling.

ZUCCHINI NOODLES WITH PESTO SAUCE

Nutrition (per serving):

- Calories: 220
- Protein: 8g
- Carbohydrates: 15g
- Fiber: 4g
- Fat: 15g

Ingredients:

- 2 large zucchinis, spiralized into noodles
- 1 cup fresh basil leaves
- 1/4 cup pine nuts
- 1/4 cup grated Parmesan cheese
- 2 cloves garlic
- Juice of 1 lemon
- 1/4 cup extra-virgin olive oil

- Salt and pepper to taste
- Cherry tomatoes, halved (for garnish)
- Grated Parmesan cheese (for garnish)

Instructions:

1. Mix the basil, pine nuts, chopped Parmesan cheese, garlic, and lemon juice in a food processor. Pulse until the food is minimal.
2. While the food processor goes, slowly pour the olive oil until the pesto is well mixed. Salt and pepper can be added to taste.
3. In a big pan, cook the zucchini noodles over medium heat for about two to three minutes or until they are just a little bit softer.
4. Put the pesto sauce in the pan and toss the zucchini noodles to cover them evenly.
5. On each plate, put some of the zucchini noodles with pesto.
6. Add cherry tomato halves and chopped Parmesan cheese as a garnish.
7. The zucchini noodles should be served right away.

BLACK BEAN AND CORN SALAD

Nutrition (per serving):

- Calories: 180
- Protein: 8g
- Carbohydrates: 32g
- Fiber: 8g
- Fat: 2g

Ingredients:

- 2 cans (15 oz each) black beans, drained and rinsed
- 1 cup corn kernels (fresh, frozen, or canned)
- 1 red bell pepper, diced
- 1/2 red onion, finely chopped
- 1 jalapeno pepper, seeded and minced (optional)
- 1/4 cup chopped fresh cilantro
- Juice of 2 limes
- 2 tablespoons extra-virgin olive oil
- 1 teaspoon ground cumin
- Salt and pepper to taste
- Avocado slices (for garnish)

Instructions:

1. Mix the black beans, corn, diced red bell pepper, chopped red onion, minced jalapeno pepper (if using), and chopped cilantro in a big bowl.
2. Mix the lime juice, extra-virgin olive oil, ground cumin, salt, and pepper in a small bowl with a whisk.
3. Pour the sauce over the mixture of black beans and toss to mix.
4. Let the salad sit for 15 to 20 minutes to combine the tastes.
5. Add avocado pieces to the black bean and corn salad before you serve it.
6. The salad should be served cold.

OATMEAL RAISIN COOKIES WITH FLAXSEEDS

Nutrition (per cookie):

- Calories: 150
- Protein: 3g
- Carbohydrates: 20g
- Fiber: 3g
- Fat: 7g

Ingredients:

- 1 cup old-fashioned oats
- 1/2 cup whole wheat flour
- 1/4 cup ground flaxseeds
- 1/2 teaspoon baking soda
- 1/2 teaspoon cinnamon
- 1/4 teaspoon salt
- 1/4 cup unsalted butter, softened
- 1/4 cup coconut oil, melted
- 1/2 cup brown sugar
- 1 egg
- 1 teaspoon vanilla extract
- 1/2 cup raisins

Instructions:

1. Turn the oven on and set it to 350°F (175°C). Put parchment paper on a baking sheet.
2. Mix the oats, whole wheat flour, ground flaxseeds, baking soda, cinnamon, and salt in a bowl with a whisk.
3. Mix the softened butter, melted coconut oil, and brown sugar in another bowl until smooth.
4. Add the egg and vanilla extract and beat until everything is well mixed.
5. Add the dry ingredients to the wet ingredients slowly until just mixed.

6. Mix the raisins in.
7. Place spoonfuls of cookie dough about 2 inches apart on the baking sheet that has been prepared.
8. Use the back of a fork to make each cookie slightly flatter.
9. Bake the cookies for 10 to 12 minutes or until the edges are golden brown.
10. Let the cookies cool for a few minutes on the baking sheet before moving them to a wire rack to cool all the way.

BARLEY AND MUSHROOM RISOTTO

Nutrition (per serving):

- Calories: 250
- Protein: 7g
- Carbohydrates: 45g
- Fiber: 8g
- Fat: 5g

Ingredients:

- 1 cup pearl barley
- 4 cups vegetable broth
- 1 tablespoon olive oil
- 1 onion, finely chopped
- 2 cloves garlic, minced
- 8 oz mushrooms, sliced
- 1/4 cup white wine (optional)
- 1/4 cup grated Parmesan cheese
- 2 tablespoons chopped fresh parsley
- Salt and pepper to taste

Instructions:

1. Bring the vegetable soup to a low boil in a pot and keep it warm.
2. Olive oil should be heated over medium heat in a large pot. Put the chopped onion in the pan and cook until it turns transparent.
3. Add the chopped mushrooms and minced garlic to the pan. Cook the mushrooms until they are golden brown and soft.
4. Add the pearl barley to the pan and stir it to coat it with the onion and mushroom mixture.
5. If you want to use it, add the white wine and cook until most of the juice is gone.
6. Add the warm veggie broth to the pan one ladle at a time. Don't stop stirring; let the liquid soak in before adding more soup.
7. Keep doing this for 25 to 30 minutes or until the barley is soft and smooth.
8. Mix in the grated Parmesan cheese and the fresh parsley that has been chopped.
9. Salt and pepper the rice to your taste.
10. The barley and vegetable risotto should be served hot.

MIXED BERRY CHIA SEED JAM

Nutrition (per 2-tablespoon serving):

- Calories: 40
- Protein: 1g
- Carbohydrates: 8g
- Fiber: 3g

- Fat: 1g

Ingredients:

- 2 cups mixed berries (such as strawberries, blueberries, raspberries, and blackberries)
- 2 tablespoons chia seeds
- 2 tablespoons honey or maple syrup (adjust to taste)
- 1 teaspoon lemon juice

Instructions:

1. Put the mixed berries in a pot and cook them over medium heat until they break down and let out their juices.
2. Use a fork or a potato masher to mash the berries to the desired consistency.
3. Mix in the honey or maple syrup, chia seeds, and lemon juice.
4. Keep cooking the mixture for another 5–10 minutes, turning it often, until it becomes thick like jam.
5. Take the pot off the burner and let the jam cool.
6. Put the mixed berry chia seed jam in a glass jar in the fridge until it is freezing and has set.
7. As the jam cools, it will get even more thick.
8. Spread the jam on toast, grits, yoghurt, or pancakes or waffles as a topping.

FIBER-RICH GRANOLA BARS

Nutrition (per bar):

- Calories: 180
- Protein: 5g

- Carbohydrates: 28g
- Fiber: 5g
- Fat: 6g

Ingredients:

- 1 1/2 cups rolled oats
- 1/2 cup chopped nuts (such as almonds, walnuts, or pecans)
- 1/2 cup dried fruit (such as raisins, cranberries, or apricots)
- 1/4 cup ground flaxseeds
- 1/4 cup honey or maple syrup
- 1/4 cup nut butter (such as almond or peanut butter)
- 1 teaspoon vanilla extract
- 1/2 teaspoon cinnamon
- Pinch of salt

Instructions:

1. Set the oven to 350°F (175°C) and put parchment paper in a baking dish.
2. Mix the rolled oats, chopped nuts, dried fruit, and ground flaxseeds in a big bowl.
3. Honey or maple syrup, nut butter, vanilla extract, cinnamon, and a pinch of salt are heated over low heat in a small pot. Stir the mixture until it is well-mixed and slightly a little bit.
4. Pour the wet mixture over the dry ingredients and stir until everything is evenly covered.
5. Put the mixture in the baking dish that you have already prepared and press it down hard to make an even layer.
6. Bake the granos for 15 to 20 minutes or until the edges are golden brown.

7. Let them all the way down before you cut them into individual bars.

SPINACH AND FETA STUFFED CHICKEN BREAST

Nutrition (per serving):

- Calories: 280
- Protein: 30g
- Carbohydrates: 5g
- Fiber: 2g
- Fat: 15g

Ingredients:

- 2 boneless, skinless chicken breasts
- 1 cup fresh spinach leaves
- 1/4 cup crumbled feta cheese
- 1/4 teaspoon garlic powder
- Salt and pepper to taste
- Olive oil for cooking

Instructions:

1. Turn the oven on and set it to 375°F (190°C).
2. Butterfly the chicken breasts by slicing them cross all the way through, then opening them like a book.
3. Sprinkle garlic powder, salt, and pepper on the inside of the chicken breasts.
4. On one side of each chicken breast, lay down the fresh spinach leaves and chopped feta cheese.

5. To cover the centre, fold the other side of the chicken breast over it.
6. Use toothpicks to hold the chicken breasts together.
7. Put olive oil in a pan and heat it over medium-high heat.
8. Brown the chicken breasts on each side for about 2 to 3 minutes.
9. Place the chicken breasts in a baking dish and bake in an oven that has already been hot for about 15 to 20 minutes or until the chicken is all through.
10. To serve, take out the toothpicks.

THREE-BEAN CHILI WITH QUINOA

Nutrition (per serving):

- Calories: 280
- Protein: 12g
- Carbohydrates: 50g
- Fiber: 12g
- Fat: 4g

Ingredients:

- 1 cup cooked quinoa
- 1 can (14 oz) diced tomatoes
- 1 can (15 oz) black beans, drained and rinsed
- 1 can (15 oz) kidney beans, drained and rinsed
- 1 can (15 oz) pinto beans, drained and rinsed
- 1 onion, chopped
- 1 bell pepper, chopped
- 2 cloves garlic, minced
- 2 tablespoons chili powder

- 1 teaspoon cumin
- 1/2 teaspoon smoked paprika
- Salt and pepper to taste
- Optional toppings: chopped green onions, shredded cheese, plain Greek yoghurt

Instructions:

1. Over medium heat, soften the chopped onion and bell pepper in a big pot.
2. Mix in the garlic that has been finely chopped, chilli powder, cumin, smoked paprika, salt, and pepper. Keep cooking for one more minute.
3. Add the chopped tomatoes with their juices, the black beans, the kidney beans, and the pinto beans to the pot. Mix it well.
4. Mix the cooked quinoa with everything else in the pot.
5. Let the chilli simmer for about 15 to 20 minutes while it occasionally lets the flavours develop.
6. Serve the three-bean chilli hot, and add toppings if you want to.

APPLE CINNAMON OVERNIGHT OATS

Nutrition (per serving):

- Calories: 250
- Protein: 8g
- Carbohydrates: 45g
- Fiber: 8g
- Fat: 4g

Ingredients:

- 1/2 cup rolled oats
- 1/2 cup unsweetened almond milk (or any milk of your choice)
- 1/4 cup Greek yogurt
- 1 small apple, diced
- 1 tablespoon chia seeds
- 1/2 teaspoon cinnamon
- 1/4 teaspoon vanilla extract
- 1 tablespoon honey or maple syrup

Instructions:

1. Mix the rolled oats, almond milk, Greek yoghurt, diced apple, chia seeds, cinnamon, and vanilla in a jar or other container.
2. Stir everything until it's all well mixed.
3. Honey or maple syrup can be drizzled over the mixture and stirred.
4. Cover the jar or other container and put it in the fridge for at least 4 hours or overnight.
5. Stir the overnight oats well before you eat them.
6. You can eat the overnight oats cold or warm them up in the oven if you want to.

LENTIL AND BROWN RICE STEW

Nutrition (per serving):

- Calories: 220
- Protein: 10g
- Carbohydrates: 40g

- Fiber: 8g
- Fat: 2g

Ingredients:

- 1 cup brown lentils, rinsed and drained
- 1/2 cup brown rice
- 1 onion, chopped
- 2 carrots, peeled and diced
- 2 celery stalks, diced
- 3 cloves garlic, minced
- 1 can (14 oz) diced tomatoes
- 6 cups vegetable broth
- 1 teaspoon dried thyme
- 1/2 teaspoon dried rosemary
- Salt and pepper to taste
- Fresh parsley, chopped (for garnish)

Instructions:

1. Over medium heat, cook the chopped onion, carrots, and celery in a bowl until soft.
2. Add the chopped garlic, thyme, and rosemary that have been dried. Keep cooking for one more minute.
3. Put the brothels, brown rice, diced tomatoes (with their juices), and veggie broth in the pot. Get it to boil.
4. Turn down the heat, cover, and let it simmer for 30–40 minutes or until the rice and lentils are soft.
5. Add salt and pepper to taste to the pot.
6. Serve the pot of lentils and brown rice hot with chopped fresh parsley on top.

AVOCADO AND BLACK BEAN WRAP

Nutrition (per serving):

- Calories: 320
- Protein: 10g
- Carbohydrates: 40g
- Fiber: 12g
- Fat: 15g

Ingredients:

- 2 whole wheat tortillas
- 1 avocado, sliced
- 1 can (15 oz) black beans, drained and rinsed
- 1 cup cooked quinoa
- 1/2 cup corn kernels (fresh, frozen, or canned)
- 1/4 cup diced red onion
- 1/4 cup chopped fresh cilantro
- Juice of 1 lime
- Salt and pepper to taste

Instructions:

1. Mix the cooked rice, black beans, corn kernels, diced red onion, chopped cilantro, lime juice, salt, and pepper in a bowl. Blend well.
2. Place the whole wheat tortillas on the table and split the avocado slices among them.
3. Spread the mixture of black beans and quinoa on the avocado pieces.
4. To make, wrap tortillas, side tortillas in and roll them tightly.
5. If you want, you can cut the wraps in half and serve them right away.

HIGH-FIBER TRAIL MIX

Nutrition (per serving, about 1/4 cup):

- Calories: 160
- Protein: 4g
- Carbohydrates: 20g
- Fiber: 5g
- Fat: 8g

Ingredients:

- 1 cup mixed nuts (such as almonds, walnuts, and cashews)
- 1/2 cup dried fruit (such as raisins, cranberries, or apricots)
- 1/4 cup pumpkin seeds
- 1/4 cup sunflower seeds
- 1/4 cup whole grain cereal
- 1/4 cup dark chocolate chips (optional)

Instructions:

1. Mix the mixed nuts, dried fruit, pumpkin seeds, sunflower seeds, whole grain cereal, and (if you're using them) dark chops together in a bowl.
2. Mix everything until it's all well blended.
3. Divide the trail mix into single-serving amounts or put it in a container that won't let air in so you can snack on it quickly.

BROCCOLI AND KALE SALAD WITH CITRUS DRESSING

Nutrition (per serving):

- Calories: 150
- Protein: 5g
- Carbohydrates: 20g
- Fiber: 6g
- Fat: 7g

Ingredients:

- 2 cups chopped broccoli florets
- 2 cups chopped kale leaves
- 1/4 cup chopped red onion
- 1/4 cup chopped almonds or walnuts
- 1/4 cup dried cranberries or raisins
- Zest and juice of 1 orange
- Zest and juice of 1 lemon
- 2 tablespoons olive oil
- 1 tablespoon honey or maple syrup
- Salt and pepper to taste

Instructions:

1. Mix the chopped broccoli leaves,ves, red onion, almonds or walnuts, and dried cranberries or raisins in a big bowl.
2. Whisk the orange zest, orange juice lemon zest, lemon juice, honey or maple syrup, and salt in a small bowl.
3. Pour the citrus dressing over the salad and toss everything together until everything is well covered.
4. Let the salad sit for ten to combine the taste.
5. The broccoli and kale salad should be served cold.

PEAR AND WALNUT BREAKFAST BOWL

Nutrition (per serving):

- Calories: 280
- Protein: 6g
- Carbohydrates: 45g
- Fiber: 8g
- Fat: 10g

Ingredients:

- 1 cup cooked quinoa
- 1 ripe pear, diced
- 1/4 cup chopped walnuts
- 1/4 cup Greek yogurt
- 1 tablespoon honey
- 1/2 teaspoon cinnamon
- 1/4 teaspoon vanilla extract

Instructions:

1. Mix the cooked quinoa, chopped pear, walnuts, Greek yoghurt, honey, cinnamon, and vanilla flavour in a bowl.
2. Stir everything until it's all well mixed.
3. The bowl of pears and walnuts can be served hot or cold.

SWEET POTATO AND BLACK BEAN ENCHILADAS

Nutrition (per serving, based on 1 enchilada):
- Calories: 280
- Protein: 10g
- Carbohydrates: 40g
- Fiber: 9g
- Fat: 9g

Ingredients:
- 4 whole wheat tortillas
- 2 cups cooked and mashed sweet potatoes
- 1 can (15 oz) black beans, drained and rinsed
- 1 cup corn kernels (fresh, frozen, or canned)
- 1 teaspoon ground cumin
- 1/2 teaspoon chilli powder
- Salt and pepper to taste
- 1 cup enchilada sauce (red or green)
- 1 cup shredded cheese (such as cheddar or Monterey Jack)

Instructions:
1. Turn the oven on and set it to 375°F (190°C).
2. Mix the mashed sweet potatoes, black beans, corn kernels, cumin powder, chilli powder, salt, and pepper in a bowl.
3. Spread the whole wheat tortillas and split the sweet potato and black bean mixture between them.
4. Roll up the tortillas and put them open-side down in a baking dish.
5. Pour enchilada sauce over the tortillas that have been rolled.
6. Shred some cheese and put it on top of the enchiladas.

7. Bake in an oven-warmed oven for about 15 to 20 minutes or until the cheese is bubbly and melted.
8. Sweet potato and black bean enchiladas should be served hot.

WHOLE-GRAIN BLUEBERRY PANCAKES

Nutrition (per serving, about two pancakes):

- Calories: 280
- Protein: 8g
- Carbohydrates: 50g
- Fiber: 7g
- Fat: 6g

Ingredients:

- 1 cup whole wheat flour
- 1/2 cup rolled oats
- 2 teaspoons baking powder
- 1/2 teaspoon cinnamon
- 1/4 teaspoon salt
- 1 cup unsweetened almond milk (or any milk of your choice)
- 1 egg
- 2 tablespoons honey or maple syrup
- 1 teaspoon vanilla extract
- 1 cup fresh or frozen blueberries

Instructions:

1. Whisk the whole wheat flour, rolled oats, baking powder, cinnamon, and salt in a bowl.
2. Mix the egg, honey maple syrup, vanilla extract, and almond milk with a whisk in another bowl.
3. Mix the wet and dry ingredients until they are just mixed.
4. Gently add the blueberries.
5. Set a pan or skillet that doesn't stick to medium heat.
6. Add about 1/4 cup of pancake batter to the pan for each pancake.
7. Cook until bubbles appear on the top, then flip and cook on the other side until both sides are golden brown.
8. Add more blueberries and honey or maple syrup to the pancakes made with whole grains and blueberries.

ROASTED BRUSSELS SPROUTS WITH BALSAMIC GLAZE

Nutrition (per serving):

- Calories: 120
- Protein: 4g
- Carbohydrates: 18g
- Fiber: 6g
- Fat: 5g

Ingredients:

- 2 cups Brussels sprouts, trimmed and halved
- 2 tablespoons olive oil
- Salt and pepper to taste
- 2 tablespoons balsamic vinegar
- 1 tablespoon honey

Instructions:

1. Set the oven to 400°F (200°C) and put parchment paper on a baking sheet.
2. Put the cut Brussels sprouts, olive oil, salt, and pepper in a bowl.
3. Spread the Brussels sprouts in one layer on the baking sheet that has been prepared.
4. Roast the Brussels sprouts in an oven that has already been warm for about 20 to 25 minutes, or until they are soft but have a little crunch.
5. Mix the balsamic vinegar and honey in a small pot. Bring to a boil and cook for a few minutes until the mixture is slightly reduced and thicker.
6. Before you serve the Brussels sprouts, drizzle the balsamic sauce over them.

CHICKPEA AND BROCCOLI STIR-FRY

Nutrition (per serving):

- Calories: 250
- Protein: 10g
- Carbohydrates: 40g
- Fiber: 10g
- Fat: 6g

Ingredients:

- 1 can (15 oz) chickpeas, drained and rinsed
- 2 cups broccoli florets
- 1 red bell pepper, sliced
- 1 carrot, julienned

- 2 cloves garlic, minced
- 2 tablespoons soy sauce
- 1 tablespoon hoisin sauce
- 1 teaspoon sesame oil
- 1/2 teaspoon ginger paste or minced ginger
- Crushed red pepper flakes (optional)
- Sesame seeds (for garnish)
- Cooked brown rice (for serving)

Instructions:

1. Some oil should be heated high in a wok or a big skillet.
2. Stir-fry the chopped garlic and ginger paste for a few seconds until the smell is pleasant.
3. Add the broccoli florets, chopped red bell pepper, and julienned carrot. Stir-fry the vegetables for about two to three minutes until they soften.
4. Add the beans that have been rinsed and drained to the wok. Stir-fry for another 2 minutes.
5. Mix the soy sauce, hoisin sauce, sesame oil, and crushed red pepper flakes (if using) in a small bowl with a whisk.
6. Pour the sauce over the vegetables and chickpeas. Stir-fry for another 1–2 minutes or until the sauce has covered everything.
7. Serve the stir-fried chickpeas and veggies over cooked brown rice, and sprinkle sesame seeds on top.

PRUNE AND WALNUT ENERGY BITES

Nutrition (per energy bite, about 1 inch in diameter):
- Calories: 100

- Protein: 2g
- Carbohydrates: 15g
- Fiber: 3g
- Fat: 4g

Ingredients:

- 1 cup pitted prunes
- 1 cup walnuts
- 1/4 cup rolled oats
- 2 tablespoons ground flaxseeds
- 1/2 teaspoon cinnamon
- Pinch of salt
- 1 tablespoon honey or maple syrup
- Unsweetened shredded coconut (for rolling, optional)

Instructions:

1. Mix the prunes with the pits taken out, walnuts, rolled oats, ground flaxseeds, cinnamon, and salt in a food processor.
2. Mix the ingredients until they stick together and form a dough.
3. Add the honey or maple syrup and process the mixture until it is well-mixed.
4. Take small amounts of the mixture and roll them into balls that are easy to eat.
5. If you want, you can roll the energy bites in chopped unsweetened coconut to cover the outside.
6. Put the energy bites on a tray lined with parchment paper and put it in the fridge for about 30 minutes to get complicated.

7. Once the energy bites are excellent, put them in an airtight container and store them in the fridge for a quick and healthy lunch.

BULGUR AND VEGETABLE STUFFED PEPPERS

Nutrition (per serving, 1 stuffed pepper):

- Calories: 220
- Protein: 8g
- Carbohydrates: 45g
- Fiber: 10g
- Fat: 2g

Ingredients:

- 4 bell peppers, any color
- 1 cup bulgur, cooked
- 1 cup mixed vegetables (such as carrots, peas, corn)
- 1 can (15 oz) black beans, drained and rinsed
- 1 teaspoon ground cumin
- 1/2 teaspoon paprika
- Salt and pepper to taste
- Chopped fresh cilantro (for garnish)

Instructions:

1. Turn the oven on and set it to 375°F (190°C).
2. Remove the seeds and skins from the bell peppers and cut off the tops.

3. Mix the cooked bulgur, the mixed veggies, the black beans, the ground cumin, the paprika, the salt, and the pepper in a bowl.
4. Put the bulgur and veggie mixture into each bell pepper.
5. Put the peppers in an oven dish and cover them with aluminium foil.
6. Bake for about 25 to 30 minutes in an oven that has already been warm or until the peppers are soft.
7. Before serving, sprinkle chopped fresh cilantro on top.

CINNAMON RAISIN QUINOA PORRIDGE

Nutrition (per serving):

- Calories: 220
- Protein: 6g
- Carbohydrates: 40g
- Fiber: 6g
- Fat: 4g

Ingredients:

- 1 cup cooked quinoa
- 1 cup unsweetened almond milk (or any milk of your choice)
- 1/4 cup raisins
- 1 tablespoon honey or maple syrup
- 1/2 teaspoon cinnamon
- 1/4 teaspoon vanilla extract
- Chopped nuts (such as almonds or walnuts) for topping

Instructions:

1. Mix the cooked quinoa, almond milk, raisins, honey or maple syrup, cinnamon, and vanilla extract in a pot.
2. Cook the mixture over medium heat, stirring occasionally, until it is warm and the raisins are plump.
3. Warm the cinnamon-raisin quinoa cereal and sprinkle chopped nuts on top.

FIBER-FULL VEGGIE BURGER

Nutrition (per serving, including bun and toppings):

- Calories: 350
- Protein: 15g
- Carbohydrates: 50g
- Fiber: 12g
- Fat: 10g

Ingredients:

- 1 can (15 oz) black beans, drained and rinsed
- 1 cup cooked quinoa
- 1/2 cup rolled oats
- 1/2 cup grated carrot
- 1/4 cup chopped onion
- 2 cloves garlic, minced
- 1 teaspoon ground cumin
- 1/2 teaspoon paprika
- Salt and pepper to taste
- Whole wheat burger buns
- Lettuce, tomato slices, red onion slices (for toppings)

Instructions:

1. Mix the cooked black beans, rolled oats, grated carrot, chopped onion, minced garlic, ground cumin, paprika, salt, and pepper in a food processor.
2. Mix the ingredients in a food processor until they come together but still have some structure.
3. Make cakes out of the mixture.
4. Heat a pan or grill to medium-high heat. Cook the veggie burgers for about 4-5 minutes on each side or until they are hot all the way through and the outside is crispy.
5. If you want, you can toast the whole wheat burger buns.
6. Put the cabbage, tomato, and red onion slices on the burgers. Serve with the sauces you like.

ROASTED RED PEPPER AND LENTIL DIP

Nutrition (per serving):

- Calories: 150
- Protein: 6g
- Carbohydrates: 25g
- Fiber: 8g
- Fat: 3g

Ingredients:

- 1 cup cooked red lentils
- 1 roasted red pepper (from a jar), drained and chopped
- 2 cloves garlic, minced
- 2 tablespoons tahini

- Juice of 1 lemon
- 1/2 teaspoon ground cumin
- Salt and pepper to taste
- Chopped fresh parsley (for garnish)

Instructions:

1. Mix the cooked red lentils, the roasted red pepper, the chopped garlic, the tahini, the lemon juice, the ground cumin, the salt, and the pepper in a food processor.
2. Process the ingredients until they are smooth and well-mixed.
3. Put the dip in a bowl for serving and top it with chopped fresh parsley.
4. Serve the roasted red pepper and lentil dip with pita chips made from whole wheat or veggie sticks.

WHOLE WHEAT PENNE WITH TOMATO BASIL SAUCE

Nutrition (per serving):

- Calories: 280
- Protein: 10g
- Carbohydrates: 50g
- Fiber: 8g
- Fat: 4g

Ingredients:

- 2 cups whole wheat penne pasta
- 1 can (14 oz) diced tomatoes
- 1/4 cup tomato paste

- 2 cloves garlic, minced
- 1/4 cup chopped fresh basil
- 1 tablespoon olive oil
- 1/2 teaspoon dried oregano
- Salt and pepper to taste
- Grated Parmesan cheese (for garnish)

Instructions:

1. Follow the directions on the package to cook the whole wheat spaghetti. Drain and put away.
2. Warm the olive oil in a pot over medium heat.
3. Add the chopped garlic and cook for about a minute or until the garlic smells good.
4. Mix the chopped tomatoes, tomato paste, dried oregano, salt, and pepper.
5. Let the sauce simmer for 10 to 15 minutes to combine the flavours.
6. Just before serving, mix in the chopped fresh basil.
7. Mix the tomato basil sauce with the cooked whole wheat noodles.
8. The pasta should be served hot with chopped Parmesan cheese on top.

HIGH-FIBER FRUIT SMOOTHIE

Nutrition (per serving):

- Calories: 200
- Protein: 5g
- Carbohydrates: 45g
- Fiber: 10g

- Fat: 3g

Ingredients:

- 1 banana
- 1/2 cup mixed berries (such as strawberries, blueberries, raspberries)
- 1/4 cup oats
- 1 tablespoon chia seeds
- 1 cup unsweetened almond milk (or any milk of your choice)
- 1/2 cup Greek yogurt
- 1 tablespoon honey or maple syrup

Instructions:

1. Blend the banana, mixed berries, oats, chia seeds, almond milk, Greek yoghurt, honey or maple syrup, and chia seeds in a blender.
2. Mix everything until it is smooth and creamy.
3. Pour the fruit drink with a lot of fibre into a glass and eat it immediately.

CRANBERRY ALMOND QUINOA SALAD

Nutrition (per serving):

- Calories: 250
- Protein: 8g
- Carbohydrates: 35g
- Fiber: 6g
- Fat: 10g

Ingredients:

- 1 cup cooked quinoa
- 1/2 cup dried cranberries
- 1/4 cup chopped almonds
- 1/4 cup chopped fresh parsley
- 2 tablespoons chopped red onion
- Juice of 1 lemon
- 2 tablespoons olive oil
- Salt and pepper to taste

Instructions:

1. Mix the cooked quinoa, the dried cranberries, the chopped nuts, the chopped fresh parsley, and the chopped red onion in a bowl.
2. Mix the lemon juice, olive oil, salt, and pepper in a small bowl with a whisk.
3. Pour the dressing over the rice mixture and toss until everything is well.
4. The cherry almond quinoa salad should be served cold.

SPICY EDAMAME SNACK

Nutrition (per serving, about 1/2 cup):

- Calories: 150
- Protein: 12g
- Carbohydrates: 10g
- Fiber: 6g
- Fat: 7g

Ingredients:

- 2 cups frozen edamame, thawed
- 1 tablespoon olive oil
- 1 teaspoon chilli powder
- 1/2 teaspoon smoked paprika
- 1/4 teaspoon cayenne pepper
- Salt to taste

Instructions:

1. Set the oven to 375°F (190°C) and put parchment paper on a baking sheet.
2. Mix the thawed edamame in a bowl with olive oil, chilli powder, smoked paprika, cayenne pepper, and salt.
3. Spread the edamame in one layer on the baking sheet that has been prepared.
4. Roast the edamame in an oven that has already been hot for about 20 to 25 minutes or until it is crispy and a little bit golden.
5. Let the hot edamame cool down a bit before you serve it.

ORANGE AND ARUGULA SALAD WITH POMEGRANATE SEEDS

Nutrition (per serving):

- Calories: 120
- Protein: 2g
- Carbohydrates: 20g
- Fiber: 4g
- Fat: 5g

Ingredients:

- 4 cups arugula leaves
- 2 oranges, peeled and segmented
- 1/2 cup pomegranate seeds
- 1/4 cup chopped walnuts
- 2 tablespoons olive oil
- 1 tablespoon balsamic vinegar
- 1 teaspoon honey
- Salt and pepper to taste

Instructions:

1. Mix the arugula leaves, orange pieces, pomegranate seeds, and chopped walnuts in a big bowl.
2. Whisk the olive oil, balsamic vinegar, honey, salt, and pepper in a small bowl.
3. Pour the dressing over the salad and toss it all together until everything is well covered.
4. The orange and lettuce salad should be served cold.

WHOLE-GRAIN RASPBERRY MUFFINS

Nutrition (per muffin):

- Calories: 180
- Protein: 5g
- Carbohydrates: 30g
- Fiber: 5g
- Fat: 5g

Ingredients:

- 1 1/2 cups whole wheat flour

- 1/2 cup rolled oats
- 1/4 cup coconut sugar or brown sugar
- 2 teaspoons baking powder
- 1/2 teaspoon cinnamon
- Pinch of salt
- 1 cup unsweetened almond milk (or any milk of your choice)
- 1/4 cup coconut oil, melted
- 1 egg
- 1 teaspoon vanilla extract
- 1 cup fresh raspberries

Instructions:

1. Set the oven to 375°F (190°C) and put paper cups in a muffin pan.
2. Mix the whole wheat flour, rolled oats, coconut sugar or brown sugar, baking powder, cinnamon, and salt in a big bowl with a whisk.
3. Mix the egg, vanilla extract, melted coconut oil, and almond milk in another bowl.
4. Pour the wet ingredients into the dry ingredients and stir until just mixed.
5. Gently add the fresh strawberries.
6. Put the same amount of batter in each muffin cup.
7. Bake the muffins in an oven that has already been heated for about 18 to 20 minutes, or until a knife stuck into the middle of a muffin comes out clean.
8. Let the muffins cool for a few minutes in the pan before moving them to a wire rack to finish cooling.

BLACK BEAN AND SWEET POTATO HASH

Nutrition (per serving):

- Calories: 280
- Protein: 8g
- Carbohydrates: 45g
- Fiber: 10g
- Fat: 8g

Ingredients:

- 2 cups cooked black beans
- 2 medium sweet potatoes, peeled and diced
- 1 red bell pepper, diced
- 1 onion, chopped
- 2 cloves garlic, minced
- 1 teaspoon ground cumin
- 1/2 teaspoon smoked paprika
- Salt and pepper to taste
- Chopped fresh cilantro (for garnish)
- Eggs (optional for serving)

Instructions:

1. Some oil should be heated in a pan over medium heat.
2. Put the chopped onion in the pan and cook until it turns transparent.
3. Add the diced sweet potatoes and cook for about 8 to 10 minutes, turning occasionally until they are slightly crispy and cooked through.
4. Add the diced red bell pepper and chopped garlic to the pan. Cook for another 2 to 3 minutes.

5. Mix in the black beans that have been cooked, cumin powder, smoked paprika, salt, and pepper.
6. Keep cooking for a few more minutes until everything is warm and mixed well.
7. You can put a fried or poached egg on top of the black bean and sweet potato dish.
8. Before serving, sprinkle chopped fresh cilantro on top.

MIXED VEGETABLE AND BARLEY SOUP

Nutrition (per serving):

- Calories: 180
- Protein: 6g
- Carbohydrates: 35g
- Fiber: 8g
- Fat: 2g

Ingredients:

- 1 cup pearl barley
- 6 cups vegetable broth
- 2 carrots, peeled and diced
- 2 celery stalks, diced
- 1 onion, chopped
- 1 bell pepper, diced
- 2 cloves garlic, minced
- 1 can (14 oz) diced tomatoes
- 1 teaspoon dried thyme
- Salt and pepper to taste
- Chopped fresh parsley (for garnish)

Instructions:

1. Mix the pearl barley and veggie broth in a large pot.
2. Bring the mixture to a boil, then turn down the heat and cook for about 20 to 25 minutes or until the barley is soft.
3. In the meantime, cook the chopped onion, diced carrots, celery, bell pepper, and minced garlic in a separate pan until the veggies are soft.
4. Add the cooked barley, broth, and veggies that have been sautéed to the pot.
5. Mix in the diced tomatoes, salt, pepper, and dried thyme.
6. Let the soup cook for another 10–15 minutes to combine the tastes.
7. Serve the hot barley and mixed veggie soup, with chopped fresh parsley.

MANGO AND BLACK BEAN QUINOA SALAD

Nutrition (per serving):

- Calories: 250
- Protein: 8g
- Carbohydrates: 45g
- Fiber: 8g
- Fat: 4g

Ingredients:

- 1 cup cooked quinoa
- 1 ripe mango, peeled and diced
- 1 can (15 oz) black beans, drained and rinsed

- 1 red bell pepper, diced
- 1/4 cup chopped red onion
- 1/4 cup chopped fresh cilantro
- Juice of 1 lime
- 2 tablespoons olive oil
- Salt and pepper to taste

Instructions:

1. Mix the cooked quinoa, chopped mango, black beans, red bell pepper, chopped red onion, and chopped fresh cilantro in a bowl.
2. Mix the lime juice, olive oil, salt, and pepper in a small bowl with a whisk.
3. Pour the dressing over the quinoa salad and toss everything together until everything is well mixed.
4. The salad with mango and black beans should be served cold.

FIBER-PACKED CHOCOLATE AVOCADO PUDDING

Nutrition (per serving):

- Calories: 180
- Protein: 4g
- Carbohydrates: 25g
- Fiber: 8g
- Fat: 9g

Ingredients:

- 2 ripe avocados, peeled and pitted

- 1/4 cup unsweetened cocoa powder
- 1/4 cup honey or maple syrup
- 1 teaspoon vanilla extract
- Pinch of salt
- Unsweetened almond milk (or any milk of your choice), as needed

Instructions:

1. Mix the ripe avocados, unsweetened cocoa powder, honey or maple syrup, vanilla extract, and a pinch of salt in a blender or food processor.
2. Mix everything until it is smooth and creamy. If you need to, add a splash of almond milk to get the consistency you want.
3. Taste it and add or take away sugar as needed.
4. Move the chocolate avocado pudding to bowls or glasses for serving.
5. Before serving the pudding, put it in the fridge for at least 30 minutes to set it.
6. Serve the pudding, which is full of grains cold.

BROCCOLI AND CHEDDAR STUFFED POTATOES

Nutrition (per serving):

- Calories: 280
- Protein: 10g
- Carbohydrates: 40g
- Fiber: 8g
- Fat: 10g

Ingredients:

- 4 medium russet potatoes
- 2 cups broccoli florets, steamed and chopped
- 1 cup shredded cheddar cheese
- 1/2 cup Greek yogurt
- Salt and pepper to taste
- Chopped fresh chives (for garnish)

Instructions:

1. Turn the oven on and set it to 400°F (200°C).
2. Scrub the russet potatoes and use a fork to poke holes in them several times.
3. Put the potatoes right on the oven rack and bake for 45 to 60 minutes, or until you can pierce them with a fork and they are soft.
4. Let the potatoes cool down, then cut off the tops and scoop the meat into a bowl.
5. Mix the cooked and chopped broccoli, shredded cheddar cheese, Greek yoghurt, salt, and pepper into the mashed potato.
6. Stuff the vegetable and cheese mixture into the potato skins.
7. Place the stuffed potatoes on a baking sheet and bake for another 10 to 15 minutes or until the cheese is melted and bubbly.
8. Before serving, sprinkle chopped fresh chives on top.

OAT AND FLAXSEED WAFFLES

Nutrition (per serving, two waffles):

- Calories: 240
- Protein: 8g
- Carbohydrates: 35g
- Fiber: 8g
- Fat: 8g

Ingredients:

- 1 cup whole wheat flour
- 1/2 cup rolled oats
- 2 tablespoons ground flaxseeds
- 1 tablespoon coconut sugar or brown sugar
- 2 teaspoons baking powder
- Pinch of salt
- 1 cup unsweetened almond milk (or any milk of your choice)
- 1/4 cup unsweetened applesauce
- 1 egg
- 1 teaspoon vanilla extract

Instructions:

1. Follow the guidelines on the box to heat the waffle iron.
2. Mix the whole wheat flour, rolled oats, ground flaxseeds, coconut sugar or brown sugar, baking powder, and salt in a big bowl with a whisk.
3. Mix the almond milk, applesauce that has yet to be sweetened, egg, and vanilla extract with a whisk in another bowl.
4. Pour the wet ingredients into the dry ingredients and stir until just mixed.
5. Use a little oil or nonstick cooking spray to grease the waffle pan.

6. Pour the waffle batter onto the waffle iron that has already been hot, and cook according to the instructions on the box.
7. Repeat with the rest of the dough.
8. Serve the oat and flaxseed waffles hot, with your favourite fruits and honey or maple syrup drizzled on top.

GRILLED PORTOBELLO MUSHROOMS WITH QUINOA

Nutrition (per serving):

- Calories: 220
- Protein: 10g
- Carbohydrates: 35g
- Fiber: 8g
- Fat: 5g

Ingredients:

- 4 large Portobello mushrooms, cleaned and stems removed
- 1 cup cooked quinoa
- 1 cup baby spinach
- 1/4 cup crumbled feta cheese
- 2 tablespoons balsamic vinegar
- 1 tablespoon olive oil
- 2 cloves garlic, minced
- Salt and pepper to taste
- Chopped fresh parsley (for garnish)

Instructions:

1. Set a grill or grill pan over medium-high heat to get it ready.
2. Mix balsamic vinegar, olive oil, chopped garlic, salt, and pepper in a bowl with the cleaned Portobello mushrooms.
3. About 4-5 minutes on each side, or until they are soft and have grill marks, is how long you should grill the mushrooms.
4. In the meantime, mix the cooked quinoa, baby spinach, and chopped feta cheese in a separate bowl.
5. After grilling the mushrooms, fill each cap with the rice mixture.
6. Before serving, sprinkle chopped fresh parsley on top.

HIGH FIBER ANTIPASTO PLATTER

Nutrition (per serving, including all components):
- Calories: 250
- Protein: 10g
- Carbohydrates: 30g
- Fiber: 12g
- Fat: 12g

Ingredients:
- Whole grain crackers or bread
- Sliced whole wheat pita
- Sliced cucumber
- Cherry tomatoes
- Sliced bell peppers
- Baby carrots
- Olives (such as Kalamata or green olives)

- Sliced cheese (such as cheddar or mozzarella)
- Hummus
- Guacamole
- Roasted red pepper dip

Instructions:

1. Place the whole grain crackers or bread, sliced whole wheat pita, sliced cucumber, cherry tomatoes, sliced bell peppers, baby carrots, olives, sliced cheese, hummus, guacamole, and roasted red pepper dip on a big platter.
2. Serve the high-fibre antipasto plate as a healthy appetizer or snack that will fill you up.

CABBAGE AND WHITE BEAN SOUP

Nutrition (per serving):

- Calories: 180
- Protein: 8g
- Carbohydrates: 30g
- Fiber: 10g
- Fat: 3g

Ingredients:

- 4 cups shredded cabbage
- 1 can (15 oz) white beans, drained and rinsed
- 1 onion, chopped
- 2 carrots, peeled and diced
- 2 cloves garlic, minced
- 6 cups vegetable broth
- 1 teaspoon dried thyme

- Salt and pepper to taste
- Chopped fresh parsley (for garnish)

Instructions:

1. In a big pot, cook the chopped onion and minced garlic until they smell good.
2. Add the chopped carrots and shredded cabbage to the pot. Cook the vegetables for a few minutes until they start to get soft.
3. Pour the vegetable soup into the pan and bring the whole thing to a boil.
4. Turn down the heat and let the veggies simmer for 15 to 20 minutes or until soft.
5. Add the white beans and dried thyme and mix well. Add 5 minutes of cooking time to warm up the beans.
6. Salt and pepper the soup to your taste.
7. Serve the cabbage and white bean soup hot, with fresh parsley that has been chopped.

RASPBERRY CHIA SEED SMOOTHIE

Nutrition (per serving):

- Calories: 200
- Protein: 5g
- Carbohydrates: 30g
- Fiber: 12g
- Fat: 8g

Ingredients:

- 1 cup frozen raspberries

- 1 banana
- 1 tablespoon chia seeds
- 1 tablespoon almond butter
- 1 cup unsweetened almond milk (or any milk of your choice)
- 1/2 cup Greek yogurt
- Honey or maple syrup (optional for sweetness)

Instructions:

1. Blend the frozen raspberries, banana, chia seeds, almond butter, almond milk, Greek yoghurt, and honey or maple syrup, if you want, in a mixer.
2. Mix everything until it is smooth and creamy.
3. Pour the raspberry chia seed smoothie into a glass and start drinking it immediately.

MEDITERRANEAN CHICKPEA SALAD

Nutrition (per serving):

- Calories: 280
- Protein: 10g
- Carbohydrates: 40g
- Fiber: 10g
- Fat: 10g

Ingredients:

- 2 cups cooked chickpeas
- 1 cup diced cucumber
- 1 cup diced tomato
- 1/2 cup chopped red onion

- 1/4 cup Kalamata olives, sliced
- 1/4 cup crumbled feta cheese
- 2 tablespoons chopped fresh parsley
- 2 tablespoons extra-virgin olive oil
- Juice of 1 lemon
- 1 teaspoon dried oregano
- Salt and pepper to taste

Instructions:

1. Mix the cooked chickpeas, diced cucumber, tomato, chopped red onion, sliced Kalamata olives, crumbled feta cheese, and chopped fresh parsley in a big bowl.
2. Mix the extra-virgin olive oil, lemon juice, dried oregano, salt, and pepper in a small bowl with a whisk.
3. Pour the sauce over the chickpea salad and toss everything together until everything is well-mixed.
4. The Mediterranean chickpea salad is best when served cold.

SPINACH AND MUSHROOM WHOLE WHEAT CALZONE

Nutrition (per serving):

- Calories: 320
- Protein: 12g
- Carbohydrates: 40g
- Fiber: 8g
- Fat: 14g

Ingredients:

- 1 pound whole wheat pizza dough
- 2 cups fresh spinach leaves
- 1 cup sliced mushrooms
- 1/2 cup ricotta cheese
- 1/2 cup shredded mozzarella cheese
- 1 clove garlic, minced
- 1 tablespoon olive oil
- 1 teaspoon dried oregano
- Salt and pepper to taste

Instructions:

1. Set the oven to 425°F (220°C) and turn it on.
2. Heat the olive oil in a pan over medium heat.
3. Add the sliced mushrooms and cook until they brown and lose water.
4. Add the chopped garlic and cook for one more minute.
5. Put the raw spinach in the pan and cook it until it shrinks. Take off the heat.
6. Roll out the whole wheat pizza dough on a greased surface into a large circle.
7. Spread the ricotta cheese on half of the dough, leaving a border around the sides.
8. On top of the ricotta, put the mushrooms and spinach cooked in butter, then add the shredded mozzarella cheese.
9. Salt and pepper the filling, and then sprinkle dried oregano on top.
10. Fold the other half of the dough over the filling and press the sides together to seal.
11. Place the calzone on a baking sheet and bake it in an oven that has been hot for about 20 to 25 minutes or until golden brown.

12. Let the calzone cool a bit before you cut it and serve it.

FIBER-RICH NUT BUTTER BALLS

Nutrition (per serving, about two balls):

- Calories: 180
- Protein: 6g
- Carbohydrates: 15g
- Fiber: 5g
- Fat: 12g

Ingredients:

- 1 cup rolled oats
- 1/2 cup nut butter (such as almond or peanut butter)
- 1/4 cup honey or maple syrup
- 1/4 cup ground flaxseeds
- 1/4 cup chopped nuts (such as almonds or walnuts)
- 1/4 cup dried cranberries or raisins
- 1 teaspoon vanilla extract
- Pinch of salt
- Unsweetened shredded coconut (for rolling, optional)

Instructions:

1. Mix the rolled oats, nut butter, honey or maple syrup, ground flaxseeds, chopped nuts, dried cranberries or raisins, vanilla extract, and a pinch of salt in a big bowl.
2. Mix everything until it's all well blended.
3. Take small amounts of the mixture and roll them into balls that are easy to eat.

4. You can coat the outside of the nut butter balls with shredded raw coconut if you want.
5. Put the balls on a tray lined with parchment paper and put it in the fridge for about 30 minutes to firm up.
6. Once the nut butter balls are cool, put them in an airtight container and store them in the fridge for a quick and healthy lunch.

BROWN RICE AND LENTIL PILAF

Nutrition (per serving):

- Calories: 250
- Protein: 8g
- Carbohydrates: 40g
- Fiber: 8g
- Fat: 6g

Ingredients:

- 1 cup brown rice
- 1/2 cup green or brown lentils
- 1 onion, chopped
- 2 carrots, peeled and diced
- 1 bell pepper, diced
- 2 cloves garlic, minced
- 1 teaspoon ground cumin
- 1/2 teaspoon ground turmeric
- 1/2 teaspoon ground coriander
- 4 cups vegetable broth
- 2 tablespoons olive oil
- Salt and pepper to taste

- Chopped fresh cilantro (for garnish)

Instructions:

1. Olive oil should be heated over medium heat in a big pot.
2. Put the chopped onion in the pan and cook until it turns transparent.
3. Dice the carrots and bell pepper and put them in the pot. Cook the vegetables for a few minutes until they start to get soft.
4. Mix in the chopped garlic, cumin powder, turmeric powder, and coriander powder. Cook for another minute or until the smell is good.
5. Put the brown rice and beans in the pot and stir them so the spices cover them.
6. Pour the vegetable soup into the pan and bring the whole thing to a boil.
7. Turn the heat to a boil, cover the pot, and cook for about 40 to 45 minutes, or until the rice and lentils are soft and the liquid has been absorbed.
8. Add salt and pepper to taste to the rice.
9. Brown rice and bean pilaf should be served hot with chopped fresh cilantro.

BLUEBERRY ALMOND OVERNIGHT OATS

Nutrition (per serving):

- Calories: 280
- Protein: 10g
- Carbohydrates: 40g

- Fiber: 8g
- Fat: 8g

Ingredients:

- 1/2 cup rolled oats
- 1/2 cup unsweetened almond milk (or any milk of your choice)
- 1/4 cup Greek yogurt
- 1/4 cup fresh or frozen blueberries
- 2 tablespoons chopped almonds
- 1 tablespoon chia seeds
- 1 tablespoon honey or maple syrup
- 1/2 teaspoon vanilla extract

Instructions:

1. Mix the rolled oats, almond milk, Greek yoghurt, blueberries, nuts chopped into small pieces, chia seeds, honey or maple syrup, and vanilla extract in a jar or other container.
2. Stir everything until it's all well mixed.
3. Close the lid and put the jar in the fridge overnight.
4. Give the oats a good stir in the morning before you eat them.

MIXED BEAN AND CORN TACOS

Nutrition (per serving, two tacos):

- Calories: 280
- Protein: 10g
- Carbohydrates: 45g

- Fiber: 10g
- Fat: 6g

Ingredients:

- 1 can (15 oz) mixed beans, drained and rinsed
- 1 cup corn kernels (fresh, frozen, or canned)
- 1 bell pepper, diced
- 1 onion, chopped
- 2 cloves garlic, minced
- 1 teaspoon ground cumin
- 1/2 teaspoon chilli powder
- Salt and pepper to taste
- 8 small whole wheat tortillas
- Sliced avocado, salsa, chopped cilantro (for toppings)

Instructions:

1. Cook the chopped onion and minced garlic in a pan until the mixture smells good.
2. Add the chopped bell pepper and pieces of corn to the pan. Cook the vegetables for a few minutes or until they are soft.
3. Add the mixed beans, cumin powder, chilli powder, salt, and pepper to the pot. Add 5 minutes of cooking time to warm up the beans.
4. The whole wheat tortillas can be heated in a dry pan or the microwave.
5. Put the tacos with a spoonful of the bean and corn filling on each tortilla.
6. Avocado slices, salsa, and chopped cilantro go on top.
7. Warm up the tacos with beans and corn.

ROASTED EGGPLANT AND QUINOA SALAD

Nutrition (per serving):

- Calories: 280
- Protein: 8g
- Carbohydrates: 40g
- Fiber: 10g
- Fat: 10g

Ingredients:

- 1 medium eggplant, diced
- 1 cup cooked quinoa
- 1 cup cherry tomatoes, halved
- 1/4 cup chopped red onion
- 1/4 cup crumbled feta cheese
- 2 tablespoons chopped fresh parsley
- 2 tablespoons extra-virgin olive oil
- Juice of 1 lemon
- 1 teaspoon dried oregano
- Salt and pepper to taste

Instructions:

1. Set the oven to 425°F (220°C) and turn it on.
2. Add olive oil, salt, and pepper to the diced eggplant.
3. Spread the eggplant on a baking sheet and roast it in an oven warmed oven for 20 to 25 minutes or until it is soft and slightly golden.
4. Mix the cooked rice, eggplant that has been roasted, cherry tomatoes, chopped red onion, crumbled feta cheese, and chopped fresh parsley in a bowl.

5. Mix the extra-virgin olive oil, lemon juice, dried oregano, salt, and pepper in a small bowl with a whisk.
6. Pour the dressing over the quinoa salad and toss everything together until everything is well mixed.
7. The eggplant and rice salad should be served cold.

APPLE WALNUT COLESLAW

Nutrition (per serving):

- Calories: 220
- Protein: 3g
- Carbohydrates: 30g
- Fiber: 6g
- Fat: 11g

Ingredients:

- 4 cups shredded green cabbage
- 1 apple, cored and thinly sliced
- 1/2 cup chopped walnuts
- 1/4 cup Greek yogurt
- 2 tablespoons mayonnaise (or olive oil for a lighter option)
- 1 tablespoon apple cider vinegar
- 1 tablespoon honey
- Salt and pepper to taste

Instructions:

1. Mix the shredded green cabbage, thinly sliced apple, and chopped walnuts in a big bowl.

2. Whisk the Greek yoghurt, mayonnaise, apple cider vinegar, honey, salt, and pepper in a small bowl.
3. Pour the dressing over the cabbage mixture and toss until everything is well covered.
4. Serve the salad with apples and walnuts cold.

WHOLE WHEAT VEGGIE PIZZA

Nutrition (per serving, one slice of pizza):

- Calories: 280
- Protein: 12g
- Carbohydrates: 40g
- Fiber: 8g
- Fat: 10g

Ingredients:

- 1 whole wheat pizza crust
- 1/2 cup tomato sauce
- 1 cup shredded mozzarella cheese
- 1 cup sliced bell peppers
- 1 cup sliced mushrooms
- 1/2 cup sliced red onion
- 1 teaspoon dried oregano
- 1 teaspoon dried basil
- Crushed red pepper flakes (optional)
- Olive oil (for drizzling)

Instructions:

1. Follow the guidelines on the pizza crust package to heat the oven.

2. Roll out the whole wheat pizza crust on a pizza stone or baking sheet.
3. Spread the tomato sauce evenly over the crust, leaving a border around the sides.
4. Cover the sauce with half of the shredded mozzarella cheese.
5. Sliced bell pepper, mushrooms, and red onion go on top of the pizza.
6. Sprinkle the veggies with the rest of the shredded mozzarella cheese.
7. You can add some crushed red pepper flakes, dried oregano and basil to the pizza.
8. Sprinkle some olive oil on top of the pizza.
9. Follow the pizza crust box instructions and bake the pizza in a preheated oven until the cheese is bubbly and melted.
10. Cut the whole wheat vegetable pizza into pieces and serve it hot.

FIBER-PACKED CHEESE AND SPINACH QUESADILLAS

Nutrition (per serving, 1 quesadilla):

- Calories: 300
- Protein: 15g
- Carbohydrates: 35g
- Fiber: 10g
- Fat: 12g

Ingredients:

- 4 whole wheat tortillas

- 2 cups fresh spinach leaves
- 1 cup shredded mozzarella cheese
- 1/2 cup black beans, drained and rinsed
- 1/4 cup diced red onion
- 1/4 cup chopped fresh cilantro
- 1 teaspoon ground cumin
- Salt and pepper to taste
- Olive oil (for cooking)

Instructions:

1. In a pan, cook the chopped red onion until it turns transparent.
2. Put the raw spinach in the pan and cook it until it shrinks. Take off the heat.
3. Mix the spinach and red onion cooked with shredded mozzarella cheese, black beans, chopped fresh cilantro, ground cumin, salt, and pepper in a bowl.
4. Put a whole wheat tortilla on a clean surface and spread half of the spinach and cheese mixture over half of it.
5. To make a half-moon form, fold the other half of the tortilla over the filling.
6. Do the same thing with the other tortillas and filling.
7. Heat a little olive oil in a pan over medium heat.
8. Cook each quesadilla for 2 to 3 minutes on each side or until the dough is crispy and the cheese is melted.
9. The cheese and spinach quesadillas should be cut in half and served hot.

SPICED PUMPKIN AND LENTIL SOUP

Nutrition (per serving):

- Calories: 220
- Protein: 10g
- Carbohydrates: 35g
- Fiber: 10g
- Fat: 5g

Ingredients:

- 1 can (15 oz) pumpkin puree
- 1 cup red lentils
- 1 onion, chopped
- 2 carrots, peeled and diced
- 2 cloves garlic, minced
- 4 cups vegetable broth
- 1 teaspoon ground cumin
- 1/2 teaspoon ground cinnamon
- 1/4 teaspoon ground nutmeg
- Salt and pepper to taste
- Greek yoghurt (for garnish)
- Chopped fresh parsley (for garnish)

Instructions:

1. In a big pot, cook the chopped onion and minced garlic until they smell good.
2. Add the diced carrots to the pot and cook for a few minutes or until they soften.
3. Add the red lentils, pumpkin puree, veggie broth, cumin, cinnamon, nutmeg, salt, and pepper to the pot.
4. Bring the mixture to a boil, then boil the heat to a simmer.
5. Cover the pot and let the soup boil for about 20 to 25 minutes, or until the lentils are soft and cooked.

6. Blend the soup until it is smooth with a hand blender. You could also put the soup in batches in a blender and blend it until it is smooth. Then, put it back in the pot.
7. Taste the food and, if necessary, change the spice.
8. Serve the pumpkin and lentil soup hot, with a dollop of Greek yoghurt and some finely chopped fresh parsley on top.

ALMOND BUTTER BANANA SANDWICH ON WHOLE GRAIN BREAD

Nutrition (per serving):
- Calories: 350
- Protein: 12g
- Carbohydrates: 45g
- Fiber: 8g
- Fat: 15g

Ingredients:
- 2 slices whole grain bread
- 2 tablespoons almond butter
- 1 banana, sliced
- 1 tablespoon chia seeds (optional)
- Honey or maple syrup (optional for drizzling)

Instructions:
1. On one side of each slice of whole grain bread, spread almond butter equally.
2. Put the banana slices on one piece of bread.
3. Put chia seeds on the banana slices

4. if you want to use them.
5. Drizzle some honey or maple syrup over the banana slices if you want.
6. Put the other slice of bread with almond butter on top to make a sandwich.
7. Gently pressing on the sandwich will help it stay together.
8. Cut the nut butter and banana sandwich in half and eat it.

BERRY SPINACH SALAD WITH FIBER-RICH VINAIGRETTE

Nutrition (per serving):

- Calories: 200
- Protein: 5g
- Carbohydrates: 25g
- Fiber: 8g
- Fat: 10g

Ingredients:

- 4 cups baby spinach leaves
- 1 cup mixed berries (such as strawberries, blueberries, and raspberries)
- 1/4 cup crumbled goat cheese or feta cheese
- 1/4 cup chopped walnuts
- 2 tablespoons extra-virgin olive oil
- 1 tablespoon balsamic vinegar
- 1 teaspoon Dijon mustard
- 1 teaspoon honey
- Salt and pepper to taste

Instructions:

1. Mix the baby spinach leaves, berries, crumbled goat or feta cheese, and chopped walnuts in a big bowl.
2. Whisk the extra-virgin olive oil, balsamic vinegar, Dijon mustard, honey, salt, and pepper in a small bowl.
3. Pour the dressing over the salad and toss it all together until everything is well covered.
4. Serve the fruit spinach salad with a vinaigrette that is full of fibre.

CRANBERRY WALNUT QUINOA STUFFED ACORN SQUASH

Nutrition (per serving):

- Calories: 280
- Protein: 8g
- Carbohydrates: 45g
- Fiber: 10g
- Fat: 10g

Ingredients:

- 2 acorn squashes, halved and seeds removed
- 1 cup cooked quinoa
- 1/2 cup dried cranberries
- 1/2 cup chopped walnuts
- 1/4 cup chopped red onion
- 1/4 cup crumbled feta cheese
- 2 tablespoons chopped fresh parsley
- 1 tablespoon olive oil

- 1 teaspoon maple syrup
- Salt and pepper to taste

Instructions:

1. Turn the oven on and set it to 375°F (190°C).
2. Place the acorn squash halves, cut side down, on a baking sheet. Bake in a warm oven for 25 to 30 minutes or until the squash is soft.
3. Mix the cooked quinoa, dried cranberries, chopped walnuts, chopped red onion, crumbled feta cheese, chopped fresh parsley, olive oil, maple syrup, salt, and pepper in a bowl.
4. Once the squash halves are cooked, flip them over and put the quinoa filling in each half.
5. Put the stuffed squash back in the oven for another 10 to 15 minutes to warm up the filling.
6. Serve the stuffed acorn squash with cranberries, walnuts, and rice hot.

GREEN PEA AND MINT HUMMUS

Nutrition (per serving):

- Calories: 160
- Protein: 5g
- Carbohydrates: 20g
- Fiber: 6g
- Fat: 7g

Ingredients:

- 1 can (15 oz) green peas, drained and rinsed

- 1/4 cup tahini
- 1/4 cup fresh mint leaves
- 2 tablespoons lemon juice
- 2 tablespoons olive oil
- 1 clove garlic
- Salt and pepper to taste
- Water (if needed)

Instructions:

1. In a food processor, combine the green peas, tahini, fresh mint leaves, lemon juice, olive oil, and garlic.
2. Mix everything until it is smooth and creamy. If the hummus is too thick, you can thin it out by adding a little water.
3. Salt and pepper the hummus to your taste.
4. Put the hummus with green peas and mint in a bowl to serve.
5. Serve the hummus with crackers made from whole grains, sliced veggies, or pita bread made from whole grains.

FIBER-RICH BANANA CHOCOLATE CHIP MUFFINS

Nutrition (per serving, 1 muffin):

- Calories: 220
- Protein: 6g
- Carbohydrates: 30g
- Fiber: 8g
- Fat: 10g

Ingredients:

- 1 1/2 cups whole wheat flour
- 1/2 cup rolled oats
- 1/2 cup coconut sugar or brown sugar
- 1/4 cup ground flaxseeds
- 1 teaspoon baking powder
- 1/2 teaspoon baking soda
- 1/2 teaspoon ground cinnamon
- Pinch of salt
- 2 ripe bananas, mashed
- 1/4 cup unsweetened applesauce
- 1/4 cup almond butter or peanut butter
- 1/4 cup unsweetened almond milk (or any milk of your choice)
- 1 teaspoon vanilla extract
- 1/2 cup dark chocolate chips

Instructions:

1. Set the oven to 350°F (175°C) and put paper cups in a muffin pan.
2. Mix the whole wheat flour, rolled oats, coconut sugar or brown sugar, ground flaxseeds, baking powder, baking soda, cinnamon powder, and salt in a big bowl with a whisk.
3. Mash the ripe bananas in another bowl and stir in the unsweetened applesauce, almond butter or peanut butter, almond milk, and vanilla extract.
4. Pour the wet ingredients into the dry ingredients and stir until just mixed.
5. Add the dark chocolate chips to the mixture.
6. Divide the batter between the muffin cups so each is about 3/4 full.

7. Bake in an oven that has already been heated for about 18 to 20 minutes or until a knife stuck into the middle of a muffin comes out clean.
8. Let the muffins cool for a few minutes in the pan, then move them to a wire rack to finish cooling.

FARRO AND ROASTED VEGETABLE MEDLEY

Nutrition (per serving):

- Calories: 280
- Protein: 8g
- Carbohydrates: 50g
- Fiber: 10g
- Fat: 6g

Ingredients:

- 1 cup farro, rinsed and drained
- 2 cups mixed vegetables (such as bell peppers, zucchini, and carrots), chopped
- 1 red onion, sliced
- 2 tablespoons olive oil
- 1 teaspoon dried thyme
- Salt and pepper to taste
- 1/4 cup crumbled feta cheese (optional)
- Chopped fresh parsley (for garnish)

Instructions:

1. Follow the directions on the package to cook the farro. When it's done, put it aside.

2. Turn the oven on and set it to 400°F (200°C).
3. Mix chopped mixed veggies and sliced red onion with dried thyme, salt, and pepper in a bowl with olive oil.
4. Spread the veggies out in an even layer on a baking sheet.
5. Roast the veggies in an oven that has already been heated for 20 to 25 minutes or until they are soft and have a bit of a caramelized flavour.
6. Mix the cooked farro and roasted veggies in a large bowl. Throw everything in.
7. If you want, you can sprinkle the mix with crumbled feta cheese.
8. Serve the farro and roasted vegetables in a warm bowl with chopped fresh parsley.

CHIA SEED AND MIXED FRUIT PARFAIT

Nutrition (per serving):

- Calories: 220
- Protein: 5g
- Carbohydrates: 35g
- Fiber: 10g
- Fat: 7g

Ingredients:

- 1/4 cup chia seeds
- 1 cup unsweetened almond milk (or any milk of your choice)
- 1 cup mixed fruits (such as berries, kiwi, and mango), chopped

- 1/4 cup granola
- 1 tablespoon honey or maple syrup

Instructions:

1. Mix the chia seeds and raw almond milk in a bowl.
2. Cover the bowl and put it in the fridge for at least 2 hours or overnight. This gives the chia seeds time to soak up the liquid and become pudding-like.
3. Stack the chia seed pudding, mixed fruits, and granola in cups or bowls.
4. Honey or maple syrup can be used to add more sweetness.
5. The chia seed and fruit mixture should be served cold.

BLACK BEAN AND CORN TOSTADAS

Nutrition (per serving, 2 tostadas):

- Calories: 280
- Protein: 10g
- Carbohydrates: 45g
- Fiber: 12g
- Fat: 8g

Ingredients:

- 8 small whole wheat tortillas
- 1 can (15 oz) black beans, drained and rinsed
- 1 cup corn kernels (fresh, frozen, or canned)
- 1 red bell pepper, diced
- 1/4 cup diced red onion
- 1/4 cup chopped fresh cilantro

- Juice of 1 lime
- 1 teaspoon ground cumin
- Salt and pepper to taste
- 1 avocado, sliced

Instructions:

1. Follow the directions on the tortilla package to heat the oven.
2. Put the whole wheat tortillas on a baking sheet and heat them in an oven that has already been turned on.
3. Mix the black beans, corn kernels, diced red bell pepper, diced red onion, chopped fresh cilantro, lime juice, ground cumin, salt, and pepper in a bowl.
4. Spread the black bean and corn filling on each warmed tortilla to combine the dish.
5. Sliced avocado should go on top.
6. Tostadas with black beans and corn should be served hot.

ASPARAGUS AND WHITE BEAN SALAD

Nutrition (per serving):
- Calories: 220
- Protein: 10g
- Carbohydrates: 30g
- Fiber: 8g
- Fat: 8g

Ingredients:
- 1 bunch asparagus, trimmed and blanched

- 1 can (15 oz) white beans, drained and rinsed
- 1 cup cherry tomatoes, halved
- 1/4 cup chopped red onion
- 1/4 cup crumbled goat cheese or feta cheese
- 2 tablespoons chopped fresh parsley
- 2 tablespoons extra-virgin olive oil
- Juice of 1 lemon
- 1 teaspoon Dijon mustard
- Salt and pepper to taste

Instructions:

1. Cut the asparagus that has been blanched into bite-sized pieces.
2. Mix the asparagus, white beans, cherry tomatoes, chopped red onion, crumbled goat or feta cheese, and chopped fresh parsley in a bowl.
3. Whisk the extra-virgin olive oil, lemon juice, Dijon mustard, salt, and pepper in a small bowl.
4. Pour the dressing over the salad and toss it all together until everything is well covered.
5. Serve the salad with white beans and asparagus cold.

HIGH FIBER OAT BRAN PANCAKES

Nutrition (per serving, about 2 pancakes):

- Calories: 250
- Protein: 10g
- Carbohydrates: 40g
- Fiber: 8g
- Fat: 6g

Ingredients:

- 1 cup oat bran
- 1/2 cup whole wheat flour
- 1 tablespoon ground flaxseeds
- 1 teaspoon baking powder
- 1/2 teaspoon ground cinnamon
- Pinch of salt
- 1 cup unsweetened almond milk (or any milk of your choice)
- 1/4 cup unsweetened applesauce
- 1 egg (or flax egg for a vegan option)
- 1 tablespoon maple syrup
- 1 teaspoon vanilla extract

Instructions:

1. Whisk the oat bran, whole wheat flour, ground flaxseeds, baking powder, cinnamon powder, and salt in a bowl.
2. Whisk the unsweetened almond milk, applesauce, egg, maple syrup, and vanilla flavour together in another bowl.
3. Pour the wet ingredients into the dry ingredients and stir until just mixed.
4. Wait a few minutes for the batter to thicken.
5. Warm up a pan or skillet that doesn't stick over medium heat and lightly grease it.
6. For each pancake, pour about 1/4 cup of batter into the pan.
7. Cook until bubbles appear on the top, then flip and cook until golden brown on the other side.
8. You can put your favourite toppings on the oat bran pancakes, such as fresh fruit, yoghurt, or maple syrup.

MEDITERRANEAN BARLEY STUFFED BELL PEPPERS

Nutrition (per serving, one stuffed bell pepper):

- Calories: 320
- Protein: 10g
- Carbohydrates: 50g
- Fiber: 12g
- Fat: 10g

Ingredients:

- 4 bell peppers, halved and seeds removed
- 1 cup cooked barley
- 1 can (15 oz) chickpeas, drained and rinsed
- 1 cup chopped tomatoes
- 1/2 cup crumbled feta cheese
- 1/4 cup chopped kalamata olives
- 2 tablespoons chopped fresh parsley
- 2 tablespoons extra-virgin olive oil
- 1 tablespoon lemon juice
- 1 teaspoon dried oregano
- Salt and pepper to taste

Instructions:

1. Turn the oven on and set it to 375°F (190°C).
2. Put the halves of bell pepper on a baking sheet.
3. Mix the cooked barley, chickpeas, chopped tomatoes, crumbled feta cheese, chopped kalamata olives, chopped

fresh parsley, extra-virgin olive oil, lemon juice, dried oregano, salt, and pepper in a bowl.
4. Fill each half of a bell pepper with a mix of rice and chickpeas.
5. When the oven is hot, bake the stuffed bell peppers for about 20 to 25 minutes or until the peppers are soft.
6. Warm up the bell peppers with rice from the Mediterranean and serve them.

ROASTED RED PEPPER AND CHICKPEA WRAP

Nutrition (per serving):

- Calories: 280
- Protein: 10g
- Carbohydrates: 45g
- Fiber: 10g
- Fat: 7g

Ingredients:

- 1 whole wheat tortilla
- 1/2 cup roasted red pepper strips (from a jar or freshly roasted)
- 1/2 cup canned chickpeas, drained and rinsed
- 1/4 cup crumbled feta cheese
- 2 tablespoons hummus
- 1 tablespoon chopped fresh parsley
- 1 teaspoon olive oil
- Juice of 1 lemon
- Salt and pepper to taste

Instructions:

1. Put the whole wheat tortilla on a clean surface.
2. Mix the roasted red pepper strips, chickpeas, crumbled feta cheese, hummus, chopped fresh parsley, olive oil, lemon juice, salt, and pepper in a bowl.
3. Put a spoonful of the mix in the middle of the tortilla.
4. Make a wrap by folding in the sides of the tortilla and rolling it up tightly.
5. The red pepper and chickpea wrap should be cut in half and served.

OAT AND FLAX BREADED BAKED CHICKEN

Nutrition (per serving):

- Calories: 280
- Protein: 30g
- Carbohydrates: 20g
- Fiber: 6g
- Fat: 10g

Ingredients:

- 4 boneless, skinless chicken breasts
- 1/2 cup oats, blended into flour
- 2 tablespoons ground flaxseeds
- 1 teaspoon paprika
- 1/2 teaspoon garlic powder
- Salt and pepper to taste
- 2 eggs, beaten

- Cooking spray

Instructions:

1. Set the oven to 375°F (190°C) and put parchment paper on a baking sheet.
2. Mix the oat flour, ground flaxseeds, paprika, garlic powder, salt, and pepper in a small dish.
3. Dip each chicken breast in the beaten eggs and let any extra drip off.
4. Coat the chicken breasts with oats and flax, pressing it on to stick.
5. Place the chicken breasts on the baking sheet that has been prepared.
6. Spray a little cooking spray on top of the chicken breasts.
7. Bake for about 25 to 30 minutes in an oven that has already been warm or until the chicken is done and the coating is crispy.
8. You can serve the baked chicken breaded with oats and flax with any side dish you want.

FIBER-PACKED BERRY SMOOTHIE BOWL

Nutrition (per serving):

- Calories: 250
- Protein: 8g
- Carbohydrates: 40g
- Fiber: 12g
- Fat: 6g

Ingredients:

- 1 cup mixed berries (such as strawberries, blueberries, and raspberries), frozen
- 1/2 banana, frozen
- 1/2 cup unsweetened almond milk (or any milk of your choice)
- 1 tablespoon chia seeds
- 1 tablespoon almond butter
- Toppings: sliced banana, granola, shredded coconut, additional berries

Instructions:

1. Mix the frozen berries, banana, unsweetened almond milk, chia seeds, and almond butter in a blender.
2. Blend until smooth and creamy. If you need to, add more almond milk for consistency.
3. The drink should go into a bowl.
4. Add sliced banana, granola, coconut shreds, and more berries.
5. Serve the fruit smoothie bowl right away. It is full of fibre.

SWEET POTATO AND LENTIL CURRY

Nutrition (per serving):

- Calories: 280
- Protein: 10g
- Carbohydrates: 45g
- Fiber: 12g
- Fat: 6g

Ingredients:

- 1 cup dry green or brown lentils, rinsed and drained
- 2 sweet potatoes, peeled and diced
- 1 onion, chopped
- 2 cloves garlic, minced
- 1 tablespoon curry powder
- 1 teaspoon ground cumin
- 1/2 teaspoon ground turmeric
- 1/4 teaspoon ground cinnamon
- 1 can (14 oz) diced tomatoes
- 1 can (13.5 oz) coconut milk
- 2 cups vegetable broth
- 2 tablespoons olive oil
- Salt and pepper to taste
- Chopped fresh cilantro (for garnish)

Instructions:

1. Olive oil should be heated over medium heat in a big pot.
2. Put the chopped onion in the pan and cook until it turns transparent.
3. Mix in the chopped garlic, curry powder, cumin powder, turmeric powder, and cinnamon powder. Cook for another minute or until the smell is good.
4. Cut up the sweet potatoes and rinse the beans. Stir them so that the spices cover them.
5. Pour in the diced tomatoes with their juices, the coconut milk, and the veggie broth.
6. Bring the mixture to a boil, then boil the heat to a simmer.
7. Cover the pot and let the curry boil for 20 to 25 minutes or until the lentils and sweet potatoes are soft.
8. Salt and pepper the curry to your taste.

9. Serve the hot lentil and sweet potato soup, with chopped fresh cilantro.

QUINOA AND BLACK BEAN STUFFED TOMATOES

Nutrition (per serving, two stuffed tomatoes):

- Calories: 250
- Protein: 10g
- Carbohydrates: 40g
- Fiber: 10g
- Fat: 6g

Ingredients:

- 4 large tomatoes
- 1 cup cooked quinoa
- 1 can (15 oz) black beans, drained and rinsed
- 1/2 cup corn kernels (fresh, frozen, or canned)
- 1/4 cup diced red onion
- 1/4 cup chopped fresh cilantro
- Juice of 1 lime
- 1 teaspoon ground cumin
- Salt and pepper to taste
- Crumbled feta cheese (optional)

Instructions:

1. Cut the tops off the tomatoes and carefully scoop out the insides, keeping the shells whole. Save the pulp from the tomato for later.

2. Mix the cooked quinoa, the black beans, the corn kernels, the diced red onion, the chopped fresh cilantro, the lime juice, the ground cumin, the salt, and the pepper in a bowl.
3. Chop up the tomato pulp you saved and add it to the rice.
4. Turn the oven on and set it to 375°F (190°C).
5. Fill the tomatoes cut open with the quinoa and black bean filling.
6. Put the tomatoes that have been put in a baking dish.
7. Bake for about 15 to 20 minutes in an oven that has already been warm or until the tomatoes are soft.
8. Before serving, you can add crumbled feta cheese over the tomatoes that have been filled.

APRICOT ALMOND ENERGY BARS

Nutrition (per serving):

- Calories: 220
- Protein: 5g
- Carbohydrates: 35g
- Fiber: 6g
- Fat: 8g

Ingredients:

- 1 cup dried apricots
- 1 cup rolled oats
- 1/2 cup almonds
- 1/4 cup ground flaxseeds
- 1/4 cup almond butter
- 2 tablespoons honey or maple syrup

- 1 teaspoon vanilla extract
- Pinch of salt

Instructions:

1. Mix well with the dried apricots, rolled oats, nuts, and ground flaxseeds in a food processor. Pulse the ingredients until they are tiny.
2. Put the almond butter, honey maple syrup, vanilla extract, and a pinch of salt in a food processor. Pulse the food again until it comes together.
3. Line a square baking dish with parchment paper, leaving a little extra so it will be easy to take out later.
4. Press the mixture firmly into the baking dish to make an even layer.
5. Put the mixture in the fridge for at least 2 hours to set.
6. Once the energy bar mix is set, lift the parchment paper from the dish.
7. Make bars or squares out of the mix.
8. Keep the apricot almond energy bars in the fridge in a container that won't let air in.

WHOLE WHEAT VEGETABLE LASAGNA

Nutrition (per serving):

- Calories: 300
- Protein: 15g
- Carbohydrates: 45g
- Fiber: 10g
- Fat: 8g

Ingredients:

- 9 whole wheat lasagna noodles
- 2 cups marinara sauce
- 1 cup low-fat ricotta cheese
- 1 cup shredded mozzarella cheese
- 1 zucchini, sliced
- 1 yellow squash, sliced
- 1 red bell pepper, sliced
- 1 cup baby spinach leaves
- 1 tablespoon olive oil
- 1 teaspoon dried basil
- 1/2 teaspoon dried oregano
- Salt and pepper to taste

Instructions:

1. Set the oven to 375°F (190°C), then cook the whole wheat lasagna noodles as directed on the box. Drain and put away.
2. Heat the olive oil in a pan over medium heat.
3. Add the zucchini, yellow squash, and red bell pepper to the pan. Sauté the veggies until they are just a little bit soft. Add salt, pepper, dried basil, and dried oregano. Take off the heat.
4. Mix half of the chopped mozzarella cheese with the low-fat ricotta cheese in a bowl.
5. Spread a thin layer of tomato sauce on the bottom of a baking dish.
6. On top of the sauce, put three cooked lasagna noodles.
7. Cover the noodles with half of the ricotta cheese filling.
8. On top of the cheese mixture, put half of the veggies that have been sautéed and half of the baby spinach leaves.

9. Repeat the layers of sauce, noodles, ricotta mixture, veggies, and spinach.
10. Put the rest of the tomato sauce and the mozzarella cheese on top.
11. Cover the baking dish with aluminium foil and bake for 20 to 25 minutes in an oven that has already been hot.
12. Take off the paper and bake for another 10 minutes or until the cheese is bubbling and melted.
13. Please wait a few minutes before cutting the lasagna and serving it.

CAULIFLOWER AND CHICKPEA STIR-FRY

Nutrition (per serving):

- Calories: 260
- Protein: 10g
- Carbohydrates: 40g
- Fiber: 12g
- Fat: 8g

Ingredients:

- 1 small head cauliflower, cut into florets
- 1 can (15 oz) chickpeas, drained and rinsed
- 2 cups broccoli florets
- 1 red bell pepper, sliced
- 1/4 cup chopped red onion
- 2 cloves garlic, minced
- 2 tablespoons soy sauce (or tamari for a gluten-free option)

- 1 tablespoon hoisin sauce
- 1 teaspoon sesame oil
- 1/2 teaspoon ground ginger
- 2 tablespoons olive oil
- Sesame seeds (for garnish)
- Chopped green onions (for garnish)

Instructions:

1. Heat the olive oil over medium-high heat in a large pan or wok.
2. Cut the garlic and red onion into small pieces and add them to the pan. For a minute, stir-fry the food until it smells good.
3. Add broccoli, cauliflower pieces, beans, and sliced red bell pepper to the pan.
4. Mix the soy sauce, hoisin sauce, sesame oil, and ground ginger in a small bowl.
5. Pour the sauce over the vegetables in the pan.
6. Stir-fry the vegetables for about 5 to 7 minutes or until they are crisp-tender.
7. Serve the broccoli and chickpea stir-fry over already-cooked brown rice or quinoa.
8. Add chopped green onions and sesame seeds to the top.

HIGH FIBER TRAIL MIX COOKIES

Nutrition (per serving, one cookie):

- Calories: 180
- Protein: 4g
- Carbohydrates: 25g
- Fiber: 6g

- Fat: 8g

Ingredients:

- 1 cup whole wheat flour
- 1/2 cup rolled oats
- 1/4 cup ground flaxseeds
- 1/2 teaspoon baking soda
- 1/4 teaspoon salt
- 1/4 cup coconut oil, melted
- 1/4 cup almond butter
- 1/2 cup coconut sugar or brown sugar
- 1 egg (or flax egg for a vegan option)
- 1 teaspoon vanilla extract
- 1/2 cup high-fibre trail mix (with nuts, seeds, and dried fruits)

Instructions:

1. Heat the oven to 350°F (175°C) and put parchment paper on a baking sheet.
2. Mix the whole wheat flour, rolled oats, ground flaxseeds, baking soda, and salt in a bowl with a whisk.
3. Whisk the melted coconut oil, almond butter, coconut sugar or brown sugar, egg, and vanilla extract together in another bowl.
4. Pour the wet ingredients into the dry ingredients and stir until just mixed.
5. Mix in the trail mix with a lot of grain.
6. Drop spoonfuls of cookie dough onto the baking sheet that has been prepared. Leave space between them.
7. Use the back of a fork to make each cookie slightly flatter.
8. Bake the cookies in an oven that has been hot for about 10 to 12 minutes or until the edges are golden brown.

9. Let the cookies cool for a few minutes on the baking sheet before moving them to a wire rack to cool all the way.

SPAGHETTI SQUASH WITH MARINARA SAUCE

Nutrition (per serving):

- Calories: 180
- Protein: 4g
- Carbohydrates: 35g
- Fiber: 8g
- Fat: 3g

Ingredients:

- 1 medium spaghetti squash
- 2 cups marinara sauce (store-bought or homemade)
- 1 tablespoon olive oil
- 2 cloves garlic, minced
- 1 teaspoon dried basil
- 1/2 teaspoon dried oregano
- Salt and pepper to taste
- Chopped fresh parsley (for garnish)
- Grated Parmesan cheese (optional)

Instructions:

1. Turn the oven on and set it to 400°F (200°C).
2. Split the spaghetti squash in half lengthwise and scoop out the seeds.
3. Olive oil, salt and pepper are put on the sides of the spaghetti squash that have been cut.

4. Put the cut side down of the spaghetti squash halves on a baking sheet.
5. Roast in an oven that has already been warm for about 40 to 45 minutes or until the squash strands are soft and can be scraped easily with a fork.
6. Make the tomato sauce while the spaghetti squash is in the oven. Warm the olive oil in a pot over medium heat.
7. Add the chopped garlic and cook for one minute or until the garlic smells good.
8. Pour the marinara sauce in and mix in the dry oregano and basil. Let the sauce cook for a little while.
9. When the spaghetti squash is done cooking, use a fork to pull the flesh apart into long strands.
10. You can top the spaghetti squash with chopped fresh parsley and sliced Parmesan cheese and serve it with marinara sauce.

THREE-BEAN AND KALE SOUP

Nutrition (per serving):

- Calories: 240
- Protein: 12g
- Carbohydrates: 40g
- Fiber: 12g
- Fat: 4g

Ingredients:

- 1 cup cooked black beans
- 1 cup cooked kidney beans
- 1 cup cooked white beans
- 1 bunch of kale, stems removed and chopped

- 1 onion, chopped
- 2 carrots, peeled and chopped
- 2 stalks celery, chopped
- 3 cloves garlic, minced
- 6 cups vegetable broth
- 1 can (14 oz) diced tomatoes
- 1 teaspoon dried thyme
- 1 teaspoon smoked paprika
- Salt and pepper to taste
- Olive oil for sautéing

Instructions:

1. Olive oil should be heated over medium heat in a big pot.
2. Chop the onion, carrots, and celery in the pot. Sauté the veggies for a few minutes until they are just a little bit softer.
3. Mix in the chopped garlic, dried thyme, and smoked paprika. Cook for another minute or until the smell is good.
4. Pour in the veggie broth and the diced tomatoes with their juices. Heat the mixture until it boils.
5. Add the black, kidney, and white beans that have already been cooked to the pot.
6. Turn the heat to a simmer and let the soup cook for 15 to 20 minutes.
7. Add the chopped kale to the pot and cook for another 5 minutes, or until the kale is soft and wilted.
8. Salt and pepper the soup to your taste.
9. The three-bean and kale soup should be served hot.

ORANGE AND ALMOND QUINOA SALAD

Nutrition (per serving):

- Calories: 280
- Protein: 8g
- Carbohydrates: 45g
- Fiber: 8g
- Fat: 8g

Ingredients:

- 1 cup cooked quinoa
- 2 oranges, peeled and segmented
- 1/2 cup sliced almonds, toasted
- 1/4 cup dried cranberries
- 1/4 cup chopped fresh mint leaves
- 2 tablespoons extra-virgin olive oil
- 1 tablespoon orange juice
- 1 teaspoon honey
- Salt and pepper to taste

Instructions:

1. Mix the cooked quinoa, orange segments, toasted almond slices, dried cranberries, and chopped fresh mint leaves in a big bowl.
2. Mix the extra-virgin olive oil, orange juice, honey, salt, and pepper in a small bowl with a whisk.
3. Pour the dressing over the rice salad and toss until everything is well covered.
4. The orange and almond quinoa salad should be served cold.

FIBER-RICH PEANUT BUTTER BANANA SMOOTHIE

Nutrition (per serving):

- Calories: 300
- Protein: 12g
- Carbohydrates: 45g
- Fiber: 10g
- Fat: 10g

Ingredients:

- 1 banana
- 2 tablespoons natural peanut butter
- 1 tablespoon ground flaxseeds
- 1 cup unsweetened almond milk (or any milk of your choice)
- 1/2 cup Greek yogurt
- 1 tablespoon honey or maple syrup (optional)
- Ice cubes

Instructions:

1. Blend the banana, natural peanut butter, ground flaxseeds, unsweetened almond milk, Greek yoghurt, and honey or maple syrup, if you want, in a blender.
2. Add ice cubes to get the thickness you want.
3. Mix until creamy and smooth.
4. Pour the peanut butter banana drink, which is full of fibre, into a glass and enjoy.

BUTTERNUT SQUASH AND LENTIL STEW

Nutrition (per serving):

- Calories: 280
- Protein: 12g
- Carbohydrates: 50g
- Fiber: 12g
- Fat: 6g

Ingredients:

- 2 cups cubed butternut squash
- 1 cup dry green or brown lentils, rinsed and drained
- 1 onion, chopped
- 2 carrots, peeled and chopped
- 2 stalks celery, chopped
- 3 cloves garlic, minced
- 6 cups vegetable broth
- 1 teaspoon ground cumin
- 1/2 teaspoon ground turmeric
- 1/2 teaspoon ground cinnamon
- Salt and pepper to taste
- Olive oil for sautéing

Instructions:

1. Olive oil should be heated over medium heat in a big pot.
2. Chop the onion, carrots, and celery in the pot. Sauté the veggies for a few minutes until they are just a little bit softer.
3. Mix in the chopped garlic, cumin powder, turmeric powder, and cinnamon powder. Cook for another minute or until the smell is good.

4. Put the cubed butternut squash and dry lentils in the pot.
5. Pour the vegetable soup into the pan and bring the whole thing to a boil.
6. Turn the heat to a boil and let the stew cook for 25 to 30 minutes, or until the lentils and butternut squash are soft.
7. Add salt and pepper to taste to the pot.
8. Serve the lentil and butternut squash stew hot.

WHOLE GRAIN CRANBERRY WALNUT SCONES

Nutrition (per serving, 1 scone):

- Calories: 220
- Protein: 6g
- Carbohydrates: 30g
- Fiber: 6g
- Fat: 10g

Ingredients:

- 2 cups whole wheat flour
- 1/4 cup coconut sugar or brown sugar
- 2 teaspoons baking powder
- 1/2 teaspoon baking soda
- 1/2 teaspoon salt
- 1/2 cup cold unsalted butter, cubed
- 1/2 cup dried cranberries
- 1/2 cup chopped walnuts
- 3/4 cup buttermilk
- 1 teaspoon vanilla extract

Instructions:

1. Set the oven to 400°F (200°C) and put parchment paper on a baking sheet.
2. Whisk the whole wheat flour, coconut sugar or brown sugar, baking powder, baking soda, and salt in a big bowl.
3. You can use a pastry cutter or your fingers to cut in the cold cubes of butter until the mixture looks like small crumbs.
4. Mix in the chopped walnuts and dried cranberries.
5. Mix the buttermilk and vanilla flavour in a separate bowl with a whisk.
6. Mix the wet and dry ingredients until they are just mixed.
7. Turn the dough onto a lightly floured surface and knead it a few times to bring it together.
8. Pat the dough into a 1-inch thick circle.
9. Make 8 wedges out of the shape.
10. Put the scones on the baking sheet that has been set up.
11. Bake the scones in an oven that has been warm for about 15 to 18 minutes or until golden brown.
12. Let the scones cool down a bit before you serve them.

CURRIED CHICKPEA AND SPINACH STUFFED PEPPERS

Nutrition (per serving, one stuffed pepper):

- Calories: 300
- Protein: 10g
- Carbohydrates: 45g
- Fiber: 10g
- Fat: 10g

Ingredients:

- 4 bell peppers, halved and seeds removed
- 1 can (15 oz) chickpeas, drained and rinsed
- 2 cups fresh baby spinach
- 1 onion, chopped
- 2 cloves garlic, minced
- 1 teaspoon curry powder
- 1/2 teaspoon ground cumin
- 1/4 teaspoon turmeric
- Salt and pepper to taste
- 1 cup cooked quinoa
- Olive oil for sautéing

Instructions:

1. Turn the oven on and set it to 375°F (190°C).
2. Put the halves of bell pepper on a baking sheet.
3. Heat some olive oil in a pan over medium heat.
4. Put the chopped onion in the pan and cook until it turns transparent.
5. Mix the chopped garlic, curry powder, ground cumin, turmeric, salt, and pepper. Cook for another minute or until the smell is good.
6. Put the chickpeas and baby spinach in the pan. Saute the spinach and chickpeas until the spinach is soft and the beans are hot.
7. Add the cooked rice to the pot.
8. Fill each half of a bell pepper with a mix of chickpeas and spinach.
9. When the oven is hot, bake the stuffed bell peppers for about 20 to 25 minutes or until the peppers are soft.
10. The stuffed peppers with chickpeas, spinach, and curry should be served hot.

BROCCOLI AND CHEESE STUFFED MUSHROOMS

Nutrition (per serving, three stuffed mushrooms):

- Calories: 180
- Protein: 10g
- Carbohydrates: 15g
- Fiber: 5g
- Fat: 10g

Ingredients:

- 12 large button mushrooms, stems removed and chopped
- 1 cup chopped broccoli florets
- 1/2 onion, chopped
- 2 cloves garlic, minced
- 1/2 cup shredded cheddar cheese
- 1/4 cup breadcrumbs
- 2 tablespoons grated Parmesan cheese
- 2 tablespoons olive oil
- Salt and pepper to taste

Instructions:

1. Set the oven to 375°F (190°C) and put parchment paper on a baking sheet.
2. Put the empty side of the mushroom caps up on the baking sheet.
3. Heat some olive oil in a pan over medium heat.
4. Add the chopped broccoli, onion, minced garlic, and mushroom stems. Saute the veggies until they are soft.

5. Take the pan off the heat and stir in the breadcrumbs and cheddar cheese.
6. Fill the vegetable and cheese mixture into each mushroom cap.
7. Grate some Parmesan cheese and sprinkle it on top of the stuffed mushrooms.
8. Bake in an oven that has been warm for about 15 to 20 minutes or until the cheese is melted and the mushrooms are cooked.
9. The broccoli and cheese-stuffed mushrooms should be served hot.

BLUEBERRY OAT BRAN MUFFINS

Nutrition (per serving, one muffin):

- Calories: 160
- Protein: 4g
- Carbohydrates: 30g
- Fiber: 6g
- Fat: 3g

Ingredients:

- 1 cup oat bran
- 1 cup whole wheat flour
- 1/2 cup coconut sugar or brown sugar
- 1 teaspoon baking powder
- 1/2 teaspoon baking soda
- 1/4 teaspoon salt
- 1 cup unsweetened almond milk (or any milk of your choice)
- 1/4 cup unsweetened applesauce

- 1 egg (or flax egg for a vegan option)
- 1 teaspoon vanilla extract
- 1 cup fresh or frozen blueberries

Instructions:

1. Set the oven to 375°F (190°C) and put paper cups in a muffin pan.
2. Mix the oat bran, whole wheat flour, coconut sugar or brown sugar, baking powder, baking soda, and salt in a bowl with a whisk.
3. Mix the almond milk, applesauce that has yet to be sweetened, egg, and vanilla extract with a whisk in another bowl.
4. Mix the wet and dry ingredients until they are just mixed.
5. Gently add the blueberries.
6. Fill each muffin cup about two-thirds of the way with the batter.
7. Bake the muffins in an oven that has already been heated for about 15 to 18 minutes, or until they are golden brown and a knife stuck in the middle comes out clean.
8. Let the muffins cool for a few minutes in the pan before moving them to a wire rack to finish cooling.

HIGH-FIBER GREEK SALAD

Nutrition (per serving):

- Calories: 220
- Protein: 8g
- Carbohydrates: 15g
- Fiber: 5g
- Fat: 15g

Ingredients:

- 2 cups mixed salad greens
- 1 cup cucumber, diced
- 1 cup cherry tomatoes, halved
- 1/2 cup red onion, thinly sliced
- 1/4 cup Kalamata olives, pitted and halved
- 1/4 cup crumbled feta cheese
- 2 tablespoons extra-virgin olive oil
- 1 tablespoon red wine vinegar
- 1 teaspoon dried oregano
- Salt and pepper to taste

Instructions:

1. Mix the salad greens, cucumber, cherry tomatoes, red onion, Kalamata olives, and crumbled feta cheese in a big bowl.
2. Mix the extra-virgin olive oil, red wine vinegar, dried oregano, salt, and pepper in a small bowl with a whisk.
3. Pour the dressing over the salad and toss it all together until everything is well covered.
4. The high-fiber Greek salad should be served cold.

MEXICAN QUINOA AND BLACK BEAN CASSEROLE

Nutrition (per serving):

- Calories: 300
- Protein: 12g
- Carbohydrates: 45g
- Fiber: 10g

- Fat: 8g

Ingredients:

- 1 cup cooked quinoa
- 1 can (15 oz) black beans, drained and rinsed
- 1 cup corn kernels (fresh, frozen, or canned)
- 1 red bell pepper, diced
- 1/2 onion, chopped
- 2 cloves garlic, minced
- 1 teaspoon chilli powder
- 1/2 teaspoon ground cumin
- 1/4 teaspoon smoked paprika
- Salt and pepper to taste
- 1 cup shredded cheddar cheese
- Chopped fresh cilantro (for garnish)
- Sliced avocado (for garnish)

Instructions:

1. Turn the oven to 375°F (190°C) and lightly grease a baking dish.
2. Heat some olive oil in a pan over medium heat.
3. Add the diced red bell pepper and chopped onion to the pan. Sauté the veggies until they are just a little bit soft.
4. Mix in the garlic that has been finely chopped, chilli powder, ground cumin, smoked paprika, salt, and pepper. Cook for another minute or until the smell is good.
5. Put the cooked quinoa, black beans, corn kernels, and half of the shredded cheddar cheese into the pan. Blend well.
6. Move the quinoa and black bean blend to the casserole dish that has been set up.
7. Sprinkle the top with the rest of the chopped cheddar cheese.

8. Bake in an oven that has already been warm for 20 to 25 minutes or until the cheese is melted and bubbly.
9. Add chopped fresh cilantro and slices of avocado to the top of the Mexican rice and black bean casserole.

FIBER-PACKED AVOCADO TOAST

Nutrition (per serving, one avocado toast):
- Calories: 250
- Protein: 8g
- Carbohydrates: 25g
- Fiber: 10g
- Fat: 15g

Ingredients:
- 2 slices whole grain bread, toasted
- 1 ripe avocado, pitted and mashed
- 1 tablespoon chia seeds
- 1 tablespoon hemp seeds
- 1 tablespoon pumpkin seeds
- 1 tablespoon sunflower seeds
- Salt and pepper to taste
- Red pepper flakes (optional)

Instructions:
1. Spread the mashed avocado on the warmed slices of whole-grain bread in an even layer.
2. Sprinkle the avocado with chia, hemp, pumpkin, and sunflower seeds.
3. If you want, you can add salt, pepper, and red pepper flakes.

4. Enjoy the avocado toast, which is full of fibre.

RED LENTIL AND SPINACH CURRY

Nutrition (per serving):
- Calories: 280
- Protein: 14g
- Carbohydrates: 45g
- Fiber: 10g
- Fat: 5g

Ingredients:
- 1 cup red lentils, rinsed and drained
- 1 onion, chopped
- 2 cloves garlic, minced
- 1 tablespoon curry powder
- 1 teaspoon ground cumin
- 1/2 teaspoon ground turmeric
- 1/4 teaspoon cayenne pepper (adjust to taste)
- 1 can (14 oz) diced tomatoes
- 2 cups vegetable broth
- 4 cups fresh baby spinach
- 1/2 cup canned coconut milk
- Salt and pepper to taste
- Olive oil for sautéing

Instructions:
1. Heat some olive oil in a pot over medium heat.
2. Put the chopped onion in the pan and cook until it turns transparent.

3. Mix in the chopped garlic, curry powder, cumin powder, turmeric powder, and cayenne pepper. Cook for another minute or until the smell is good.
4. Put the red lentils, diced tomatoes with their juices, and veggie broth in the pot.
5. Bring the mixture to a boil, then boil the heat to a simmer. Cover the lentils and cook for 15 to 20 minutes or until soft.
6. Add the fresh baby spinach to the soup and let it wilt.
7. Pour the coconut milk in a can and stir until everything is well-mixed.
8. Salt and pepper the red lentil and spinach soup to your taste.
9. Serve the soup over brown rice or quinoa that has been cooked.

SPINACH AND QUINOA STUFFED BELL PEPPERS

Nutrition (per serving, one stuffed pepper):

- Calories: 250
- Protein: 10g
- Carbohydrates: 40g
- Fiber: 8g
- Fat: 5g

Ingredients:

- 4 bell peppers, halved and seeds removed
- 1 cup cooked quinoa
- 2 cups fresh baby spinach

- 1 onion, chopped
- 2 cloves garlic, minced
- 1/2 cup crumbled feta cheese
- 1/4 cup chopped fresh parsley
- 2 tablespoons olive oil
- Salt and pepper to taste

Instructions:

1. Turn the oven on and set it to 375°F (190°C).
2. Put the halves of bell pepper on a baking sheet.
3. Heat some olive oil in a pan over medium heat.
4. Put the chopped onion in the pan and cook until it turns transparent.
5. Add the diced garlic and continue cooking for another minute.
6. Put the fresh baby spinach in the pan and cook it until soft.
7. Mix the cooked quinoa, the spinach and onion mixture that has been sautéed, the crumbled feta cheese, the chopped fresh parsley, the salt, and the pepper in a bowl.
8. Fill each half of a bell pepper with rice and spinach.
9. When the oven is hot, bake the stuffed bell peppers for about 20 to 25 minutes or until the peppers are soft.
10. Serve the bell peppers stuffed with spinach and rice hot.

ALMOND COCONUT CHIA SEED PUDDING

Nutrition (per serving):
- Calories: 280

- Protein: 8g
- Carbohydrates: 25g
- Fiber: 10g
- Fat: 18g

Ingredients:

- 1/4 cup chia seeds
- 1 cup unsweetened almond milk (or any milk of your choice)
- 2 tablespoons almond butter
- 2 tablespoons shredded coconut
- 1 tablespoon honey or maple syrup
- 1/2 teaspoon vanilla extract
- Sliced almonds and additional shredded coconut for topping

Instructions:

1. Whisk the chia seeds and unsweetened almond milk together in a bowl.
2. Add the almond butter, coconut shreds, honey or maple syrup, and vanilla extract. Blend well.
3. Cover the bowl and put it in the fridge for at least 2 hours or overnight until the chia seeds have soaked up the liquid and the mixture has thickened.
4. Give the chia seed pudding a good stir before you serve it.
5. Put the pudding in cups or bowls to serve.
6. Add sliced almonds and chopped coconut to the top.

WHOLE WHEAT VEGGIE CALZONE

Nutrition (per serving, 1 calzone):

- Calories: 320
- Protein: 12g
- Carbohydrates: 45g
- Fiber: 8g
- Fat: 10g

Ingredients:

- 1 pound whole wheat pizza dough
- 1 cup part-skim mozzarella cheese, shredded
- 1 cup mixed vegetables (bell peppers, zucchini, mushrooms, etc.), sautéed
- 1/4 cup marinara sauce
- 1 teaspoon dried oregano
- Olive oil for brushing
- Flour for dusting

Instructions:

1. Set the oven to 400°F (200°C) and put parchment paper on a baking sheet.
2. Make sure each piece of pizza dough is the same size.
3. Roll out each piece of dough into a circle on a clean surface.
4. On one half of each bread circle, spread marinara sauce.
5. Shredded mozzarella cheese, sautéed mixed veggies, and dried oregano go on top of the sauce.
6. Making a half-moon shape, fold the other half of the dough over the toppings.
7. Use a fork to crimp and seal the sides of the dough by pressing them together.
8. Put the calzones on the baking sheet that has been set up.
9. Olive oil should be used to coat the sides of the calzones.
10. Bake the calzones in an oven that has already been warm for about 20 to 25 minutes or until golden brown.

11. Let the calzones cool down a bit before you serve them.

FIBER-RICH TROPICAL FRUIT SALAD

Nutrition (per serving):

- Calories: 180
- Protein: 2g
- Carbohydrates: 45g
- Fiber: 8g
- Fat: 1g

Ingredients:

- 2 cups mixed tropical fruits (pineapple, mango, papaya, kiwi, etc.), diced
- 1 banana, sliced
- 1/4 cup unsweetened shredded coconut
- 2 tablespoons chia seeds
- 1 tablespoon honey or maple syrup
- Fresh mint leaves for garnish

Instructions:

1. Mix the diced tropical fruits and the sliced banana in a bowl.
2. Mix the shredded unsweetened coconut, chia seeds, and honey or maple syrup in a small bowl.
3. Pour the chia seed mixture over the berries and toss it all together gently.
4. Let the fruit salad sit for about ten to fifteen minutes to combine the tastes.
5. Before serving, sprinkle with fresh mint leaves.

BARLEY AND LENTIL VEGETABLE STIR-FRY

Nutrition (per serving):

- Calories: 280
- Protein: 10g
- Carbohydrates: 45g
- Fiber: 12g
- Fat: 5g

Ingredients:

- 1 cup cooked barley
- 1/2 cup cooked green or brown lentils
- 2 cups mixed vegetables (bell peppers, carrots, broccoli, etc.), sliced
- 1/4 cup low-sodium soy sauce
- 2 tablespoons sesame oil
- 1 tablespoon rice vinegar
- 1 teaspoon grated fresh ginger
- 2 cloves garlic, minced
- 1 tablespoon sesame seeds
- Chopped green onions for garnish

Instructions:

1. Heat the sesame oil on high in a wok or a big skillet.
2. Stir-fry the sliced vegetables for a few minutes until they are crisp-tender.
3. Stir in the cooked barley and beans and toss everything together.

4. Mix the low-sodium soy sauce, rice vinegar, fresh ginger, and crushed garlic in a bowl with a whisk.
5. Pour the sauce into the pan with the barley and lentils. Stir-fry for another 2–3 minutes to make sure everything is hot.
6. Add sesame seeds to the stir-fry and mix them in.
7. Before serving, sprinkle chopped green onions on top.

BLACK BEAN AND AVOCADO TACOS

Nutrition (per serving, two tacos):

- Calories: 280
- Protein: 10g
- Carbohydrates: 45g
- Fiber: 12g
- Fat: 8g

Ingredients:

- 1 can (15 oz) black beans, drained and rinsed
- 1 avocado, sliced
- 1 cup shredded lettuce
- 1/2 cup diced tomatoes
- 1/4 cup diced red onion
- 1/4 cup chopped fresh cilantro
- Juice of 1 lime
- 1 teaspoon ground cumin
- 1/2 teaspoon chilli powder
- Salt and pepper to taste
- Whole wheat tortillas

Instructions:

1. Mash the black beans with a fork in a bowl. Mix in the cumin, chilli powder, salt, and pepper that have been ground.
2. Mix the diced tomatoes, red onion, chopped fresh cilantro, lime juice, salt, and pepper in a separate bowl. The salsa will be this.
3. Warm up the whole wheat tortillas.
4. To make the tacos, spread a layer of mashed black beans on each tortilla.
5. Place avocado slices, leaf shreds, and a spoonful of salsa on top.
6. Make tacos out of the dough and serve.

ROASTED BEET AND CHICKPEA SALAD

Nutrition (per serving):

- Calories: 220
- Protein: 8g
- Carbohydrates: 35g
- Fiber: 8g
- Fat: 6g

Ingredients:

- 2 medium beets, peeled and diced
- 1 can (15 oz) chickpeas, drained and rinsed
- 4 cups mixed salad greens
- 1/4 cup crumbled goat cheese or feta cheese
- 1/4 cup chopped walnuts
- 2 tablespoons balsamic vinegar

- 1 tablespoon olive oil
- 1 teaspoon honey
- Salt and pepper to taste

Instructions:

1. Set the oven to 400°F (200°C) and put parchment paper on a baking sheet.
2. Spread the diced beets in a single layer on the baking sheet. Roast the beets for 20 to 25 minutes or until soft and slightly browned.
3. Mix the roasted beets, chickpeas, salad leaves, crumbled goat or feta cheese, and chopped walnuts in a bowl.
4. Whisk the balsamic vinegar, olive oil, honey, salt, and pepper in a small bowl.
5. Pour the dressing over the salad and toss it all together until everything is well covered.
6. Serve the beet and chickpea salad that has been cooked.

HIGH-FIBER APPLE CINNAMON PANCAKES

Nutrition (per serving, two pancakes):

- Calories: 280
- Protein: 10g
- Carbohydrates: 45g
- Fiber: 8g
- Fat: 8g

Ingredients:

- 1 cup whole wheat flour

- 1/2 cup oat bran
- 2 teaspoons baking powder
- 1 teaspoon ground cinnamon
- 1/4 teaspoon salt
- 1 cup unsweetened almond milk (or any milk of your choice)
- 1/4 cup unsweetened applesauce
- 1 egg (or flax egg for a vegan option)
- 1 apple, peeled, cored, and grated
- Olive oil or cooking spray for cooking

Instructions:

1. Whisk the whole wheat flour, oat bran, baking powder, cinnamon powder, and salt in a bowl.
2. Whisk together the chopped apple, almond milk, unsweetened applesauce, and egg in another bowl.
3. Mix the wet and dry ingredients until they are just mixed.
4. Heat a nonstick pan or grill over medium heat and lightly oil or spray it with cooking or olive oil.
5. For each pancake, pour about 1/4 cup of batter into the pan.
6. Cook the pancake until bubbles appear on the top, then flip it and cook for another 1–2 minutes or until golden brown.
7. Repeat with the rest of the dough.
8. Warm up the apple cinnamon pancakes that are high in fibre.

MEDITERRANEAN BULGUR SALAD

Nutrition (per serving):

- Calories: 250
- Protein: 8g
- Carbohydrates: 40g
- Fiber: 10g
- Fat: 6g

Ingredients:

- 1 cup cooked bulgur
- 1 cup diced cucumber
- 1 cup cherry tomatoes, halved
- 1/2 cup diced red onion
- 1/4 cup Kalamata olives, pitted and halved
- 1/4 cup crumbled feta cheese
- 2 tablespoons chopped fresh parsley
- 2 tablespoons extra-virgin olive oil
- 1 tablespoon lemon juice
- 1 teaspoon dried oregano
- Salt and pepper to taste

Instructions:

1. Mix the cooked bulgur, diced cucumber, cherry tomatoes, red onion, Kalamata olives, crumbled feta cheese, and chopped fresh parsley.
2. Mix the extra-virgin olive oil, lemon juice, dried oregano, salt, and pepper in a small bowl with a whisk.
3. Pour the dressing over the bulgur salad and toss it all together until everything is well covered.
4. The Mediterranean bulgur salad is best when served cold.

ROASTED VEGETABLE AND HUMMUS WRAP

Nutrition (per serving):

- Calories: 280
- Protein: 10g
- Carbohydrates: 40g
- Fiber: 10g
- Fat: 10g

Ingredients:

- 1 whole wheat tortilla
- 1/4 cup hummus
- 1/2 cup mixed roasted vegetables (bell peppers, zucchini, eggplant, etc.)
- 1/4 cup baby spinach leaves
- 1/4 cup shredded carrot
- 1 tablespoon chopped fresh herbs (such as basil, parsley, or cilantro)
- Salt and pepper to taste

Instructions:

1. Spread the hummus over the whole wheat bread in an even layer.
2. On top of the hummus, layer the roasted mixed veggies, baby spinach leaves, shredded carrot, and chopped fresh herbs.
3. Add salt and pepper to taste.
4. As you roll the tortilla up, fold the sides as you go.
5. The wrap should be cut in half and served.

FIBER-PACKED WALNUT RAISIN COOKIES

Nutrition (per serving, 1 cookie):

- Calories: 120
- Protein: 3g
- Carbohydrates: 15g
- Fiber: 4g
- Fat: 6g

Ingredients:

- 1 cup whole wheat flour
- 1/2 cup rolled oats
- 1/4 cup chopped walnuts
- 1/4 cup raisins
- 1/4 cup coconut oil, melted
- 1/4 cup honey or maple syrup
- 1 egg (or flax egg for a vegan option)
- 1 teaspoon vanilla extract
- 1/2 teaspoon baking soda
- 1/4 teaspoon salt
- 1/2 teaspoon ground cinnamon

Instructions:

1. Heat the oven to 350°F (175°C) and put parchment paper on a baking sheet.
2. Mix the whole wheat flour, rolled oats, chopped walnuts, raisins, baking soda, salt, and cinnamon powder in a bowl.
3. Mix the honey or maple syrup, egg, vanilla extract, and melted coconut oil in another bowl.
4. Mix the wet and dry ingredients until they are well mixed.

5. Drop spoonfuls of cookie dough onto the baking sheet that has been prepared. Leave space between them.
6. Use the back of a fork to make each cookie slightly flatter.
7. Bake the cookies in an oven that has been hot for about 10 to 12 minutes or until golden brown.
8. Let the cookies cool for a few minutes on the baking sheet before moving them to a wire rack to cool all the way.

LENTIL AND MUSHROOM SHEPHERD'S PIE

Nutrition (per serving):
- Calories: 300
- Protein: 12g
- Carbohydrates: 45g
- Fiber: 10g
- Fat: 8g

Ingredients:
- 2 cups cooked green or brown lentils
- 1 onion, chopped
- 2 cloves garlic, minced
- 2 cups sliced mushrooms
- 1 cup diced carrots
- 1 cup frozen peas
- 1 cup vegetable broth
- 2 tablespoons tomato paste
- 1 teaspoon dried thyme
- Salt and pepper to taste
- 4 cups mashed sweet potatoes

Instructions:

1. Turn the oven on and set it to 375°F (190°C).
2. Heat some olive oil in a pan over medium heat.
3. Put the chopped onion in the pan and cook until it turns transparent.
4. Add the diced garlic and continue cooking for another minute.
5. Slice the mushrooms and cut the carrots into small pieces. Saute the veggies until they are soft.
6. Mix in the cooked lentils, frozen peas, veggie broth, tomato paste, dried thyme, salt, and pepper. Just keep cooking for a few more minutes until everything is hot.
7. Move the lentils and vegetables to an oven-safe dish.
8. Spread the mashed sweet potatoes on top in an even layer.
9. Bake in an oven that has already been hot for 20 to 25 minutes or until the shepherd's pie is warm and the sweet potato topping is golden.
10. Let the shepherd's pie cool down a bit before you serve it.

QUINOA AND VEGETABLE STUFFED PORTOBELLO MUSHROOMS

Nutrition (per serving, two stuffed mushrooms):

- Calories: 220
- Protein: 10g
- Carbohydrates: 35g
- Fiber: 8g
- Fat: 5g

Ingredients:

- 4 large Portobello mushrooms, stems removed
- 1 cup cooked quinoa
- 1 cup mixed vegetables (bell peppers, zucchini, onion, etc.), diced and sautéed
- 1/4 cup crumbled goat cheese or feta cheese
- 2 tablespoons chopped fresh parsley
- 1 tablespoon balsamic vinegar
- 1 tablespoon olive oil
- Salt and pepper to taste

Instructions:

1. Set the oven to 375°F (190°C) and put parchment paper on a baking sheet.
2. Place the Portobello mushrooms, gill side up, on the baking sheet.
3. Mix the cooked quinoa, diced and sautéed mixed veggies, crumbled goat cheese or feta cheese, chopped fresh parsley, balsamic vinegar, olive oil, salt, and pepper in a bowl.
4. Fill the caps of the Portobello mushrooms with the quinoa and veggie mix.
5. Bake in an oven heated for about 15 to 20 minutes or until the mushrooms are soft and the sauce is hot.
6. The Portobello mushrooms stuffed with rice and vegetables should be served warm.

MIXED BERRY CHIA SEED SMOOTHIE

Nutrition (per serving):

- Calories: 250
- Protein: 8g
- Carbohydrates: 40g
- Fiber: 12g
- Fat: 6g

Ingredients:

- 1 cup mixed berries (strawberries, blueberries, raspberries, etc.), fresh or frozen
- 1 banana
- 1 tablespoon chia seeds
- 1 tablespoon almond butter
- 1 cup unsweetened almond milk (or any milk of your choice)
- 1/2 cup water
- 1 teaspoon honey or maple syrup (optional)

Instructions:

1. Mix the berries, banana, chia seeds, almond butter, unsweetened almond milk, water, and honey or maple syrup, if you want, in a blender.
2. Mix until creamy and smooth.
3. Pour the mixed berry chia seed smoothie into cups and enjoy it.

CAULIFLOWER AND WHITE BEAN MASH

Nutrition (per serving):

- Calories: 150

- Protein: 6g
- Carbohydrates: 25g
- Fiber: 8g
- Fat: 4g

Ingredients:

- 1 head cauliflower, chopped into florets
- 1 can (15 oz) white beans, drained and rinsed
- 2 cloves garlic, minced
- 2 tablespoons olive oil
- 1/4 cup unsweetened almond milk (or any milk of your choice)
- Salt and pepper to taste
- Chopped fresh parsley for garnish

Instructions:

1. Steam or boil the florets of cauliflower until they are soft.
2. Heat the olive oil in a pan over medium heat. Add the chopped garlic and cook it until it smells good.
3. Mix the cooked cauliflower, white beans, garlic that has been sautéed, unsweetened almond milk, salt, and pepper in a food processor.
4. If more almond milk is needed, process until smooth and creamy.
5. Serve the hot mashed cauliflower and white beans, with chopped fresh parsley.

WHOLE WHEAT MARGHERITA PIZZA

Nutrition (per serving, 1 slice - makes 8 slices total):

- Calories: 220

- Protein: 10g
- Carbohydrates: 30g
- Fiber: 5g
- Fat: 7g

Ingredients:

- 1 whole wheat pizza dough (store-bought or homemade)
- 1/2 cup tomato sauce
- 1 cup part-skim mozzarella cheese, shredded
- 1 cup cherry tomatoes, halved
- 1/4 cup fresh basil leaves
- 2 cloves garlic, minced
- 1 tablespoon olive oil
- Salt and pepper to taste

Instructions:

1. Follow the steps on the pizza dough to heat the oven.
2. Roll out the whole wheat pizza dough on a greased surface until it's as thick as you want.
3. Put the dough on a pizza stone or baking sheet rolled out.
4. Spread the tomato sauce on the dough, leaving a border around the sides.
5. Shred the mozzarella cheese and sprinkle it on top of the sauce.
6. Place the halves of cherry tomatoes on top of the cheese.
7. Sprinkle the chopped garlic, salt, and pepper on the pizza, then drizzle it with olive oil.
8. Bake the pizza in a preheated oven according to the dough guidelines or until the crust is golden and the cheese is melted.
9. Take it out of the oven and put fresh basil leaves on top.
10. Slice the Margherita pizza made with whole wheat and serve.

SPICED CHICKPEA AND KALE STEW

Nutrition (per serving):

- Calories: 250
- Protein: 10g
- Carbohydrates: 40g
- Fiber: 12g
- Fat: 5g

Ingredients:

- 1 can (15 oz) chickpeas, drained and rinsed
- 4 cups chopped kale leaves
- 1 onion, chopped
- 2 cloves garlic, minced
- 1 can (14 oz) diced tomatoes
- 4 cups vegetable broth
- 1 teaspoon ground cumin
- 1/2 teaspoon ground coriander
- 1/4 teaspoon ground turmeric
- 1/4 teaspoon cayenne pepper (adjust to taste)
- Salt and pepper to taste
- 1 tablespoon olive oil
- Juice of 1 lemon
- Chopped fresh cilantro for garnish

Instructions:

1. Heat the olive oil in a pot over medium heat.
2. Put the chopped onion in the pan and cook until it turns transparent.

3. Mix in the garlic that has been finely chopped, cumin, coriander, turmeric, and cayenne pepper. Cook for another minute or until the smell is good.
4. Add the chopped kale leaves and cook them until they become soft.
5. Pour the diced tomatoes and veggie broth into the pan. Get it to boil.
6. Put the beans in the pot and boil the heat to a simmer.
7. Let the stew cook for 15 to 20 minutes to combine the tastes.
8. Salt, pepper, and lemon juice are used to flavour the stew.
9. Serve the chickpea and kale stew with fresh chopped cilantro on top.

FIBER-RICH TRAIL MIX ENERGY BITES

Nutrition (per serving, two energy bites - makes about 12 bites total):

- Calories: 180
- Protein: 5g
- Carbohydrates: 25g
- Fiber: 6g
- Fat: 7g

Ingredients:

- 1 cup old-fashioned rolled oats
- 1/2 cup natural peanut butter
- 1/3 cup honey or maple syrup
- 1/4 cup ground flaxseeds

- 1/4 cup chopped nuts (almonds, walnuts, etc.)
- 1/4 cup dried fruit (raisins, cranberries, etc.)
- 1/4 cup dark chocolate chips
- 1 teaspoon vanilla extract
- Pinch of salt

Instructions:

1. Mix the rolled oats, natural peanut butter, honey or maple syrup, ground flaxseeds, chopped nuts, dried fruit, dark chocolate chips, vanilla extract, and a pinch of salt in a big bowl.
2. Mix well until all of the ingredients are well blended.
3. Put the mixture in the fridge for 20–30 minutes to make it easier to work with.
4. Use your hands to roll the mixture into small balls that are easy to eat.
5. Put the energy bites on a tray lined with parchment paper and put it in the fridge for another 30 minutes to set.
6. Once the energy bites are hard, put them in a container that won't let air in and put it in the fridge.

GRILLED VEGGIE AND HUMMUS PANINI

Nutrition (per serving - makes 2 panini):

- Calories: 280
- Protein: 10g
- Carbohydrates: 40g
- Fiber: 8g
- Fat: 10g

Ingredients:

- 4 slices whole wheat bread
- 1/2 cup hummus
- 1 zucchini, sliced
- 1 red bell pepper, sliced
- 1 yellow bell pepper, sliced
- 1 red onion, sliced
- 1 tablespoon olive oil
- Salt and pepper to taste

Instructions:

1. Heat a grill pan or sandwich press.
2. Mix the sliced zucchini, red bell pepper, yellow bell pepper, and red onion with salt and pepper and olive oil in a bowl.
3. Slice the veggies and grill them until they are soft and have grill marks.
4. On each piece of whole wheat bread, spread hummus.
5. To make sandwiches, put the grilled veggies between two slices of bread.
6. Put the sandwiches in the panini press or grill pan and cook until the bread is warmed and the filling is hot.
7. Cut the sandwich with grilled vegetables and hummus in half and serve.

SWEET POTATO AND BLACK BEAN TACOS

Nutrition (per serving, 2 tacos):

- Calories: 250

- Protein: 8g
- Carbohydrates: 40g
- Fiber: 10g
- Fat: 6g

Ingredients:

- 4 small whole wheat tortillas
- 2 cups cooked and mashed sweet potatoes
- 1 can (15 oz) black beans, drained and rinsed
- 1 cup shredded lettuce
- 1/2 cup diced tomatoes
- 1/4 cup diced red onion
- 1/4 cup chopped fresh cilantro
- Juice of 1 lime
- 1 teaspoon ground cumin
- 1/2 teaspoon chilli powder
- Salt and pepper to taste

Instructions:

1. Warm up the whole wheat tortillas.
2. Mix ground cumin, chilli powder, salt, and pepper with mashed sweet potatoes.
3. Mix the black beans, tomatoes, red onion, chopped fresh cilantro, lime juice, salt, and pepper in another bowl.
4. To make the tacos, spread a layer of mashed sweet potatoes on each tortilla.
5. You can put black bean salsa, lettuce shreds, and more cilantro on top.
6. Make tacos out of the dough and serve.

HIGH-FIBER RASPBERRY ALMOND MUFFINS

Nutrition (per serving, one muffin - makes 12 muffins total):

- Calories: 220
- Protein: 6g
- Carbohydrates: 35g
- Fiber: 8g
- Fat: 8g

Ingredients:

- 2 cups whole wheat flour
- 1/2 cup almond flour
- 1/2 cup rolled oats
- 1/4 cup ground flaxseeds
- 1 teaspoon baking powder
- 1/2 teaspoon baking soda
- 1/2 teaspoon salt
- 1 teaspoon ground cinnamon
- 1/2 cup honey or maple syrup
- 1/4 cup unsweetened applesauce
- 1/4 cup almond butter
- 1 cup unsweetened almond milk (or any milk of your choice)
- 1 teaspoon vanilla extract
- 1 cup fresh or frozen raspberries
- 1/2 cup chopped almonds

Instructions:

1. Set the oven to 375°F (190°C) and put paper cups in a muffin pan.

2. Mix the whole wheat flour, almond flour, rolled oats, ground flaxseeds, baking powder, baking soda, salt, and ground cinnamon in a big bowl with a whisk.
3. Whisk the honey or maple syrup, unsweetened applesauce, almond butter, unsweetened almond milk, and vanilla flavour in another bowl.
4. Mix the wet and dry ingredients until they are just mixed.
5. Add the raspberries and chopped nuts in a gentle way.
6. Put the same amount of batter in each muffin cup.
7. Bake in an oven that has already been heated for about 18 to 20 minutes or until a knife stuck into the middle of a muffin comes out clean.
8. Let the muffins cool for a few minutes in the pan before moving them to a wire rack to finish cooling.

TOMATO AND BLACK BEAN QUINOA BOWL

Nutrition (per serving):
- Calories: 300
- Protein: 12g
- Carbohydrates: 45g
- Fiber: 10g
- Fat: 8g

Ingredients:
- 1 cup cooked quinoa
- 1 can (15 oz) black beans, drained and rinsed
- 1 cup diced tomatoes
- 1/2 cup diced red onion

- 1/4 cup chopped fresh cilantro
- 1 avocado, sliced
- Juice of 1 lime
- 1 teaspoon ground cumin
- Salt and pepper to taste

Instructions:

1. Mix the cooked quinoa, black beans, tomatoes, red onion, chopped fresh cilantro, sliced avocado, lime juice, ground cumin, salt, and pepper in a bowl.
2. Throw everything together and mix it well.
3. The quinoa, tomatoes, and black beans bowl should be served at room temperature.

BROCCOLI AND CARROT SLAW

Nutrition (per serving):

- Calories: 80
- Protein: 3g
- Carbohydrates: 15g
- Fiber: 5g
- Fat: 1g

Ingredients:

- 2 cups broccoli florets, finely chopped
- 1 cup shredded carrots
- 1/4 cup chopped red onion
- 1/4 cup chopped fresh parsley
- 2 tablespoons sunflower seeds
- 2 tablespoons raisins or dried cranberries
- 2 tablespoons plain Greek yogurt

- 1 tablespoon apple cider vinegar
- 1 teaspoon honey
- Salt and pepper to taste

Instructions:

1. Mix together the broccoli pieces that have been finely chopped, the shredded carrots, the chopped red onion, the chopped fresh parsley, the sunflower seeds, and the raisins or dried cranberries.
2. Whisk the plain Greek yoghurt, apple cider vinegar, honey, salt, and pepper in a separate bowl.
3. Pour the sauce over the broccoli and carrots and toss until everything is coated.
4. Let the slaw sit for 10 to 15 minutes to combine the tastes.
5. Serve the carrot and broccoli sauce.

SPAGHETTI SQUASH WITH LENTIL MARINARA

Ingredients:

- 1 medium spaghetti squash
- 1 cup green or brown lentils, cooked and drained
- 2 cups marinara sauce (store-bought or homemade)
- 1 tablespoon olive oil
- 2 cloves garlic, minced
- 1 teaspoon dried oregano
- Salt and pepper to taste
- Fresh basil leaves for garnish

Instructions:

1. Turn the oven on and set it to 400°F (200°C).
2. Split the spaghetti squash in half lengthwise and scoop out the seeds.
3. Olive oil the cut sides of the squash and put them on a baking sheet with the cut side down.
4. Roast the squash in an oven that has already been heated for about 40 to 50 minutes or until the skin is soft enough to shred easily with a fork.
5. Make the lentil marinara sauce while the squash is cooking. Olive oil is heated in a pot over medium heat. Add the chopped garlic and cook for about a minute or until the garlic smells good.
6. Cook the lentils and then add them and the tomato sauce to the pan. Mix in salt, pepper, and dry oregano. Let it cook for 10 to 15 minutes.
7. When the spaghetti squash is done, use a fork to pull the flesh apart into pieces that look like spaghetti.
8. Serve the spaghetti squash with lentil marinara sauce on top and fresh basil leaves on the side as a topping.

Nutrition (per serving):

- Calories: ~300
- Protein: ~15g
- Carbohydrates: ~55g
- Fiber: ~12g
- Fat: ~5g

THREE-BEAN AND QUINOA SALAD

Ingredients:

- 1 cup quinoa, rinsed

- 2 cups water or vegetable broth
- 1 can (15 oz) black beans, drained and rinsed
- 1 can (15 oz) kidney beans, drained and rinsed
- 1 can (15 oz) chickpeas, drained and rinsed
- 1 red bell pepper, diced
- 1 cup fresh parsley, chopped
- 1/2 red onion, finely chopped
- 1 cup cherry tomatoes, halved
- Juice of 2 lemons
- 3 tablespoons olive oil
- 2 teaspoons ground cumin
- Salt and pepper to taste

Instructions:

1. Mix rice and water or vegetable broth in a medium saucepan. Bring to a boil, turn the heat down to low, cover, and simmer for 15 to 20 minutes, until quinoa is cooked and liquid is absorbed. Use a fork to fluff it up, then let it cool.
2. Cooked quinoa, black beans, kidney beans, chickpeas, diced red bell pepper, chopped parsley, finely chopped red onion, and halved cherry tomatoes are mixed in a big bowl.
3. Mix lemon juice, olive oil, ground cumin, salt, and pepper in a small bowl with a whisk to make the sauce.
4. The dressing goes on top of the rice and beans. Toss well to mix everything and cover it with the dressing.
5. Serve the salad cold as the main course or as a side dish.

Nutrition (per serving):

- Calories: ~380
- Protein: ~15g
- Carbohydrates: ~60g

- Fiber: ~14g
- Fat: ~10g

ROASTED RED PEPPER AND HUMMUS WRAP

Ingredients:

- 4 whole-wheat or spinach tortillas
- 1 cup hummus (store-bought or homemade)
- 2 large roasted red peppers, sliced
- 2 cups baby spinach leaves
- 1 small cucumber, julienned
- 1 medium carrot, julienned
- 1/2 red onion, thinly sliced

Instructions:

1. Set the tortillas out on a clean table.
2. Spread about 1/4 cup of hummus on each tortilla, leaving a border around the sides.
3. On top of the hummus, layer thin slices of roasted red pepper, baby spinach leaves, julienned cucumber, julienned carrot, and thin pieces of red onion.
4. To make a wrap, fold the sides of the tortilla in and roll it tight from the bottom.
5. Cut the wraps in half across the middle and serve.

Nutrition (per serving):

- Calories: ~300
- Protein: ~9g
- Carbohydrates: ~40g

- Fiber: ~10g
- Fat: ~12g

HIGH FIBER ZUCCHINI BREAD

Ingredients:

- 2 cups grated zucchini
- 1 1/2 cups whole wheat flour
- 1/2 cup oats
- 1/2 cup chopped walnuts or pecans
- 1/4 cup ground flaxseed
- 1 teaspoon baking powder
- 1/2 teaspoon baking soda
- 1 teaspoon ground cinnamon
- 1/2 teaspoon ground nutmeg
- 1/2 teaspoon salt
- 2 large eggs
- 1/4 cup honey or maple syrup
- 1/4 cup plain Greek yogurt
- 1/4 cup unsweetened applesauce
- 1 teaspoon vanilla extract

Instructions:

1. Turn the oven on and set it to 350°F (175°C)—grease or line with parchment paper a loaf pan.
2. Mix the whole wheat flour, oats, chopped nuts, ground flaxseed, baking powder, baking soda, cinnamon, nutmeg, and salt in a large bowl.
3. Whisk together the eggs, honey or maple syrup, Greek yoghurt, applesauce, and vanilla extract until everything is well mixed.

4. Mix the wet and dry ingredients until they are just mixed. Refrain from mixing too much.
5. Mix the chopped zucchini into the batter until it is spread out evenly.
6. Pour the batter into the loaf pan that has already been greased and smooth the top.
7. Bake for 45 to 50 minutes, or until a toothpick in the middle comes out clean.
8. Let the zucchini bread cool in the pan for about 10 minutes, then move it to a wire rack to cool fully before slicing.

Nutrition (per serving):

- Calories: ~180
- Protein: ~6g
- Carbohydrates: ~25g
- Fiber: ~4g
- Fat: ~7g

MOROCCAN LENTIL AND VEGETABLE STEW

Ingredients:

- 1 cup green or brown lentils, uncooked
- 1 tablespoon olive oil
- 1 onion, chopped
- 2 carrots, peeled and diced
- 2 bell peppers, diced
- 3 cloves garlic, minced
- 1 teaspoon ground cumin

- 1 teaspoon ground coriander
- 1/2 teaspoon ground turmeric
- 1/2 teaspoon ground cinnamon
- 1/4 teaspoon cayenne pepper (adjust to taste)
- 1 can (15 oz) diced tomatoes
- 4 cups vegetable broth
- 1 cup chopped spinach or kale
- Salt and pepper to taste
- Fresh cilantro leaves for garnish
- Lemon wedges for serving

Instructions:

1. Rinse the lentils with cold water and put them to the side.
2. Olive oil should be heated over medium heat in a big pot. Add the chopped onion, diced carrots, and sliced bell peppers. Sauté the veggies for about 5–7 minutes or until they get soft.
3. Mix the chopped garlic, ground cumin, coriander, turmeric, cinnamon, and cayenne pepper. Cook for another 1–2 minutes until the food smells good.
4. Mix in the diced tomatoes and beans that have yet to be cooked.
5. Pour the vegetable soup into the pan and bring the whole thing to a boil. Turn the heat down to low, cover the pot, and let the stew boil for about 25 to 30 minutes or until the lentils are soft.
6. Add the chopped spinach or kale to the pot and stir until it wilts.
7. Salt and pepper can be added to taste.
8. The Moroccan lentil and veggie stew should be served with lemon wedges and fresh cilantro leaves on top.

Nutrition (per serving):

- Calories: ~250
- Protein: ~12g
- Carbohydrates: ~45g
- Fiber: ~15g
- Fat: ~3g

STUFFED BELL PEPPERS WITH FARRO AND FETA

Ingredients:

- 4 large bell peppers, any colour
- 1 cup farro, uncooked
- 2 cups vegetable broth
- 1 tablespoon olive oil
- 1 onion, chopped
- 2 cloves garlic, minced
- 1 zucchini, diced
- 1 cup diced tomatoes (canned or fresh)
- 1 teaspoon dried oregano
- 1 teaspoon dried basil
- 1/2 cup crumbled feta cheese
- Salt and pepper to taste
- Fresh parsley for garnish

Instructions:

1. Turn the oven on and set it to 375°F (190°C).
2. Remove the seeds and skins from the bell peppers and cut off the tops. Put away.
3. Mix the farro and the veggie broth in a medium saucepan. Bring to a boil, boil the heat to low, cover, and simmer for

20 to 25 minutes or until the farro is soft. Pour out any extra liquid.

4. Olive oil should be heated over medium heat in a large pot. Add the chopped onion and cook for about 3 to 4 minutes or until the onion becomes transparent.

5. Add the chopped zucchini and sliced garlic to the pan. Keep cooking for 3–4 minutes or until the zucchini is soft.

6. Mix the chopped tomatoes, dried oregano, dried basil, cooked farro, and half of the crumbled feta cheese. Cook for a few more minutes so the tastes can come together. Salt and pepper can be added to taste.

7. Stuff the bell peppers with the farro mixture and put them in a baking dish.

8. Spread the rest of the chopped feta cheese on top of the peppers that have been filled.

9. Cover the baking dish with aluminium foil and bake in a warm oven for 25 to 30 minutes or until the peppers are soft.

10. Add some fresh parsley as a garnish before serving.

Nutrition (per serving):

- Calories: ~350
- Protein: ~12g
- Carbohydrates: ~60g
- Fiber: ~10g
- Fat: ~8g

KIWI AND CHIA SEED BREAKFAST BOWL

Ingredients:

- 2 kiwi fruits, peeled and sliced
- 2 tablespoons chia seeds
- 1 cup Greek yoghurt (plain or vanilla)
- 1/4 cup granola
- 1 tablespoon honey or maple syrup (optional)
- Fresh mint leaves, for garnish

Instructions:

1. Mix the chia seeds and 1/2 cup of water in a small bowl. Stir it well and let it sit for about 15 to 20 minutes until the chia seeds have soaked up the liquid and made a gel-like substance.
2. Stack Greek yoghurt, chia seed gel, and sliced kiwi in bowls to serve.
3. If you want, you can add granola and honey or maple syrup on top.
4. Add some fresh mint leaves to the top.
5. Have the bowl of food right away.

Nutrition (per serving):

- Calories: ~300
- Protein: ~12g
- Carbohydrates: ~45g
- Fiber: ~10g
- Fat: ~8g

FIBER-PACKED MEDITERRANEAN SALAD

Ingredients:

- 2 cups cooked quinoa
- 1 can (15 oz) chickpeas, drained and rinsed
- 1 cup diced cucumber
- 1 cup diced tomatoes
- 1/2 cup diced red onion
- 1/2 cup chopped Kalamata olives
- 1/4 cup crumbled feta cheese
- 1/4 cup chopped fresh parsley
- 1/4 cup chopped fresh mint
- Juice of 1 lemon
- 3 tablespoons extra-virgin olive oil
- 1 teaspoon dried oregano
- Salt and pepper to taste

Instructions:

1. Mix the cooked quinoa, chickpeas, cucumber, tomatoes, red onion, chopped Kalamata olives, crumbled feta cheese, chopped parsley, and chopped mint in a big bowl.
2. Mix the lemon juice, extra-virgin olive oil, dried oregano, salt, and pepper in a small bowl with a whisk.
3. Pour the sauce over the salad and mix it well.
4. The Mediterranean salad is a healthy and light meal.

Nutrition (per serving):

- Calories: ~320
- Protein: ~10g
- Carbohydrates: ~45g
- Fiber: ~10g
- Fat: ~12g

BARLEY AND LENTIL STUFFED ZUCCHINI

Ingredients:

- 4 medium zucchini
- 1/2 cup pearl barley, rinsed
- 1/2 cup green or brown lentils, rinsed
- 2 cups vegetable broth
- 1 tablespoon olive oil
- 1 onion, chopped
- 2 cloves garlic, minced
- 1 carrot, diced
- 1 bell pepper, diced
- 1 teaspoon dried thyme
- 1 teaspoon dried rosemary
- Salt and pepper to taste
- Grated Parmesan cheese, for garnish (optional)

Instructions:

1. Turn the oven on and set it to 375°F (190°C).
2. Half the zucchini lengthwise and scoop out the seeds to make a hole in the middle.
3. Mix the pearl barley, the lentils, and the veggie broth in a medium saucepan. Bring to a boil, turn the heat down to low, cover, and cook for about 25 to 30 minutes, or until the barley and lentils are soft. Pour out any extra liquid.
4. Olive oil should be heated over medium heat in a large pot. Add the chopped onion and cook for about 3 to 4 minutes or until the onion becomes transparent.
5. Add the chopped garlic, carrot, and bell pepper to the pan. Cook for 5–7 minutes more or until the veggies are soft.

6. Mix in the cooked barley, lentils, thyme, rosemary, salt, and pepper. Cook for a few more minutes so the tastes can come together.
7. Fill the holes in the zucchini halves with the barley and bean mixture.
8. Cover the stuffed zucchini with aluminium foil and put it in a baking dish. Bake for about 25 to 30 minutes in an oven that has already been warm or until the zucchini is soft.
9. Grated Parmesan cheese can be sprinkled on the stuffed zucchini before serving.

Nutrition (per serving):
- Calories: ~280
- Protein: ~10g
- Carbohydrates: ~50g
- Fiber: ~12g
- Fat: ~5g

BLACK BEAN AND CORN SALSA

Ingredients:
- 1 can (15 oz) black beans, drained and rinsed
- 1 cup corn kernels (fresh, frozen, or canned)
- 1/2 cup diced red onion
- 1 cup diced tomatoes
- 1/4 cup chopped fresh cilantro
- Juice of 1 lime
- 1 tablespoon olive oil
- 1 teaspoon ground cumin
- 1/2 teaspoon chilli powder

- Salt and pepper to taste
- Optional: diced jalapeño for extra heat

Instructions:

1. Mix the black beans, corn, red onion, tomatoes, and chopped cilantro in a big bowl.
2. Mix the lime juice, olive oil, ground cumin, chilli powder, salt, and pepper in a small bowl with a whisk to make the sauce.
3. The sauce goes on top of the beans and corn. Toss them together well.
4. If you want more heat and taste, you can add diced jalapeno.
5. Serve the black bean and corn salsa as a cool dip with tortilla chips or as a topping for salads, wraps, or grilled meats.

Nutrition (per serving):

- Calories: ~120
- Protein: ~5g
- Carbohydrates: ~20g
- Fiber: ~5g
- Fat: ~3g

WHOLE WHEAT VEGGIE STROMBOLI

Ingredients:

- 1 whole wheat pizza dough (store-bought or homemade)
- 1 cup tomato sauce
- 1 cup shredded mozzarella cheese
- 1 cup sliced bell peppers
- 1 cup sliced mushrooms

- 1/2 cup sliced red onion
- 1/2 cup sliced black olives
- 1 teaspoon dried oregano
- 1 teaspoon dried basil
- Salt and pepper to taste

Instructions:

1. Turn the oven on and set it to 400°F (200°C).
2. Roll out the pizza dough into a rectangle on a lightly oiled surface.
3. Spread the tomato sauce on the dough, leaving a border around the sides.
4. On top of the tomato sauce, layer the shredded mozzarella, sliced bell peppers, sliced mushrooms, red onion, and black olives on top of the tomato sauce.
5. Add salt, pepper, dried oregano, and dried basil to the veggies.
6. Roll the dough carefully around the veggies and cheese to make a log.
7. Place the stromboli seam-side down on a baking sheet covered with parchment paper.
8. Bake in an oven that has already been warm for 20 to 25 minutes, or until the crust is golden brown and the cheese is melted.
9. Please wait a few minutes before cutting the stromboli and serving it.

Nutrition (per serving):

- Calories: ~300
- Protein: ~15g
- Carbohydrates: ~40g
- Fiber: ~6g
- Fat: ~10g

FIBER-RICH CHOCOLATE AVOCADO SMOOTHIE

Ingredients:

- 1 ripe avocado, peeled and pitted
- 1 ripe banana
- 1 cup spinach leaves
- 1 tablespoon cocoa powder
- 1 tablespoon chia seeds
- 1 cup almond milk (or any milk of choice)
- 1 tablespoon honey or maple syrup (optional)
- Ice cubes

Instructions:

1. Blend the avocado, banana, spinach leaves, cocoa powder, chia seeds, almond milk, and honey or maple syrup (if using) in a blender.
2. Blend until the mixture is smooth and creamy, adding ice cubes as needed to get the right texture.
3. Taste it and add or take away sugar as needed.
4. Pour the smoothie right into cups and drink it right away.

Nutrition (per serving):

- Calories: ~250
- Protein: ~5g
- Carbohydrates: ~35g
- Fiber: ~12g
- Fat: ~14g

BUTTERNUT SQUASH AND BLACK BEAN ENCHILADAS

Ingredients:

- 2 cups butternut squash, peeled and cubed
- 1 can (15 oz) black beans, drained and rinsed
- 1 cup diced bell peppers
- 1/2 cup diced red onion
- 2 cloves garlic, minced
- 1 teaspoon ground cumin
- 1/2 teaspoon chilli powder
- Salt and pepper to taste
- 8 whole wheat tortillas
- 1 1/2 cups enchilada sauce (store-bought or homemade)
- 1 cup shredded cheddar cheese
- Fresh cilantro for garnish

Instructions:

1. Turn the oven on and set it to 375°F (190°C).
2. Spread the butternut squash cubes on a baking sheet and drizzle olive oil over them. When the oven is hot, roast the squash for about 20 to 25 minutes or until soft.
3. Heat olive oil in a pan over medium heat. Add the chopped red onion, chopped bell peppers, and crushed garlic. Sauté the veggies for about 3 to 4 minutes until they start to get soft.
4. Put the ground cumin, chilli powder, salt, and pepper in the pan with the black beans. Cook for another 2–3 minutes to bring the flavours together.
5. Mix the roasted butternut squash and the black bean mixture in a big bowl.

6. Spread a thin layer of enchilada sauce on the bottom of a baking dish.
7. Put some butternut squash and black beans in each whole wheat tortilla. Roll up and put seam-side down in the baking dish.
8. Pour the rest of the enchilada sauce over the tortillas that have been filled.
9. Shred some cheddar cheese and put it on top.
10. Bake in an oven that has already been warm for 20 to 25 minutes or until the cheese is melted and bubbly.
11. Before serving, sprinkle fresh cilantro on top.

Nutrition (per serving):

- Calories: ~350
- Protein: ~15g
- Carbohydrates: ~50g
- Fiber: ~12g
- Fat: ~10g

QUINOA AND KALE STUFFED ACORN SQUASH

Ingredients:

- 2 acorn squash, halved and seeds removed
- 1 cup quinoa, rinsed
- 2 cups vegetable broth
- 2 cups chopped kale
- 1/2 cup dried cranberries
- 1/2 cup chopped pecans
- 1/4 cup crumbled goat cheese
- 2 tablespoons olive oil
- 1 tablespoon balsamic vinegar

- Salt and pepper to taste

Instructions:

1. Turn the oven on and set it to 375°F (190°C).
2. Put the cut sides of the acorn squash halves on a baking sheet. Add some olive oil and salt and pepper to taste.
3. When the oven is hot, roast the acorn squash for about 40 to 45 minutes or until the meat is soft.
4. Mix the quinoa and veggie broth in a medium saucepan. Bring to a boil, then boil the heat to low, cover, and simmer for 15 to 20 minutes, or until the quinoa is cooked and the liquid is absorbed.
5. Mix the cooked quinoa, chopped kale, dried cranberries, chopped pecans, crumbled goat cheese, olive oil, and balsamic vinegar in a big bowl. Toss the ingredients well to mix them and cover them with the sauce.
6. Fill each half of the roasted acorn squash with rice and kale.
7. Put the stuffed acorn squash halves back in the oven for about 10 minutes to heat everything.
8. The stuffed acorn squash with quinoa and kale is a healthy and hearty.

Nutrition (per serving):

- Calories: ~350
- Protein: ~9g
- Carbohydrates: ~50g
- Fiber: ~8g
- Fat: ~15g

ALMOND CRANBERRY ENERGY BITES

Ingredients:

- 1 cup rolled oats
- 1/2 cup almond butter
- 1/3 cup honey or maple syrup
- 1/2 cup chopped almonds
- 1/2 cup dried cranberries
- 1/4 cup ground flaxseed
- 1 teaspoon vanilla extract
- Pinch of salt

Instructions:

1. Mix rolled oats, almond butter, honey or maple syrup, chopped almonds, dried cranberries, ground flaxseed, vanilla extract, and a pinch of salt in a big bowl.
2. Mix well until all of the ingredients are spread out equally.
3. Put the mixture in the fridge for 20–30 minutes to let it harden.
4. Once the dough has cooled, take a spoonful and roll it into bite-sized balls.
5. Put the energy bites on a parchment-paper-lined baking sheet.
6. Put the energy bites back in the fridge for another 30 minutes to set.
7. Once the energy bites are set, put them in a sealed container and put it in the fridge.
8. Energy bites with almonds and cranberries are a quick and healthy snack.

Nutrition (per serving, about 2 energy bites):

- Calories: ~180

- Protein: ~5g
- Carbohydrates: ~20g
- Fiber: ~4g
- Fat: ~10g

SPINACH AND MUSHROOM WHOLE WHEAT PASTA

Ingredients:

- 8 oz whole wheat pasta (such as penne or spaghetti)
- 2 cups fresh spinach leaves
- 1 cup sliced mushrooms
- 1/2 cup diced onion
- 2 cloves garlic, minced
- 2 tablespoons olive oil
- 1/4 cup grated Parmesan cheese
- Juice of 1 lemon
- Salt and pepper to taste
- Red pepper flakes (optional)

Instructions:

1. Follow the directions on the package to cook the whole wheat pasta. Drain and put away.
2. Olive oil is heated over medium heat in a large pot. Add the chopped onion and mushroom slices. Sauté the veggies for about 5–7 minutes or until soft.
3. Add the garlic that has been chopped and the fresh spinach leaves to the pan. Cook for 2–3 minutes or until the spinach has turned limp.

4. Put the cooked pasta in the pan with the veggies and toss it all together.
5. Sprinkle the pasta and veggies with the lemon juice. Add salt, pepper, and, if you want, red pepper flakes to taste.
6. Grate some Parmesan cheese and sprinkle it over the pasta. Toss again to mix.
7. Whole wheat pasta with spinach and mushrooms is a tasty and filling meal.

Nutrition (per serving):
- Calories: ~350
- Protein: ~10g
- Carbohydrates: ~50g
- Fiber: ~8g
- Fat: ~10g

HIGH-FIBER MIXED BERRY PANCAKES

Ingredients:
- 1 cup whole wheat flour
- 1 tablespoon ground flaxseed
- 1 tablespoon chia seeds
- 1 teaspoon baking powder
- 1/2 teaspoon baking soda
- 1/4 teaspoon salt
- 1 cup buttermilk (or milk of choice)
- 1 large egg
- 2 tablespoons honey or maple syrup

- 1 cup mixed berries (blueberries, raspberries, strawberries)
- Butter or oil for cooking

Instructions:

1. Whisk the whole wheat flour, ground flaxseed, chia seeds, baking powder, baking soda, and salt in a big bowl.
2. Whisk the buttermilk, egg, and honey or maple syrup in another bowl.
3. Pour the wet ingredients into the dry ingredients and stir until just mixed. Don't mix the batter too much; a few lumps are fine.
4. Gently mix in the berries.
5. Heat a pan or grill over medium heat and lightly grease it with butter or oil.
6. For each pancake, pour 1/4 cup of batter into the pan.
7. Cook the pancake until bubbles appear on the top, then flip it and cook for another 1–2 minutes until golden brown.
8. Repeat with the rest of the dough.
9. Serve the high-fibre pancakes with more berries and honey or maple syrup drizzled on top.

Nutrition (per serving, about two pancakes):

- Calories: ~250
- Protein: ~8g
- Carbohydrates: ~40g
- Fiber: ~6g
- Fat: ~6g

RATATOUILLE WITH BROWN RICE

Ingredients:

- 1 eggplant, diced
- 2 zucchinis, diced
- 1 red bell pepper, diced
- 1 yellow bell pepper, diced
- 1 onion, diced
- 3 cloves garlic, minced
- 2 cups diced tomatoes (canned or fresh)
- 1 teaspoon dried thyme
- 1 teaspoon dried oregano
- 1/2 teaspoon dried basil
- Salt and pepper to taste
- 2 cups cooked brown rice
- Fresh parsley for garnish

Instructions:

1. Olive oil is heated over medium heat in a large pot. Add the diced eggplant and cook for about 5 to 7 minutes, until the eggplant has softened and turned a little brown. Take out of the pan and set away.
2. Suppose you need to add more olive oil to the same pan. Add the chopped zucchini and cook for about 4 to 5 minutes, until the zucchini is brown and soft. Take out and put away.
3. Do the same thing with the diced red and yellow bell peppers, cooking them for about 3–4 minutes or until they are just a little bit softer.
4. Suppose you need to add more olive oil to the same pan. The chopped onion should be cooked for 3–4 minutes until transparent.
5. Add the chopped garlic and cook for another minute or until the garlic smells good.

6. Return the cooked eggplant, zucchini, and bell peppers to the pan. Add the chopped tomatoes, salt, pepper, dried thyme, dried oregano, dried basil, and dried thyme.
7. Let the ratatouille cook for 15 to 20 minutes to blend the flavours.
8. Serve the ratatouille with cooked brown rice and fresh parsley on top.

Nutrition (per serving):

- Calories: ~300
- Protein: ~8g
- Carbohydrates: ~55g
- Fiber: ~12g
- Fat: ~5g

CHICKPEA AND SPINACH STUFFED PORTOBELLO MUSHROOMS

Ingredients:

- 4 large Portobello mushrooms, stems removed
- 1 can (15 oz) chickpeas, drained and rinsed
- 2 cups chopped spinach
- 1/2 cup diced red onion
- 2 cloves garlic, minced
- 1 teaspoon ground cumin
- 1/2 teaspoon smoked paprika
- Salt and pepper to taste
- 1/2 cup crumbled feta cheese
- Olive oil for drizzling
- Fresh parsley for garnish

Instructions:

1. Turn the oven on and set it to 375°F (190°C).
2. Place the Portobello mushrooms, gill side up, on a baking sheet.
3. Heat olive oil in a pan over medium heat. Add the chopped red onion and cook for about 3 to 4 minutes until the onion becomes transparent.
4. Add the chopped spinach and sliced garlic to the pan. Cook for 2–3 minutes or until the spinach has turned limp.
5. Mix well with the beans, cumin powder, smoked paprika, salt, and pepper. Cook for a few more minutes so the tastes can come together.
6. Spread the chickpea and spinach mixture into the gills of the Portobello mushrooms.
7. Crumble feta cheese and put it on top of the stuffed mushrooms.
8. Pour olive oil over the mushrooms to keep them from sticking together.
9. Bake in an oven that has already been warm for 20 to 25 minutes or until the cheese is melted and the mushrooms are soft.
10. Add some fresh parsley as a garnish before serving.

Nutrition (per serving):

- Calories: ~250
- Protein: ~12g
- Carbohydrates: ~35g
- Fiber: ~9g
- Fat: ~8g

MIXED BERRY CHIA SEED PARFAIT

Ingredients:

- 1 cup mixed berries (blueberries, raspberries, strawberries)
- 1 tablespoon chia seeds
- 1 cup Greek yoghurt (plain or vanilla)
- 1/4 cup granola
- Honey or maple syrup for drizzling (optional)
- Mint leaves, for garnish

Instructions:

1. With a fork, mash the mixed berries in a bowl to make a berry sauce that has some chunks.
2. Stir in the chia seeds and let the mixture sit for about 10 to 15 minutes to let the chia seeds soak up the liquid and thicken the compote.
3. Stack the chia seed berry sauce, Greek yoghurt, and granola in glasses or bowls.
4. If you want, drizzle with honey or maple syrup.
5. Add mint leaves to the top.
6. The mixed berry and chia seed salad is a healthy and tasty snack.

Nutrition (per serving):

- Calories: ~250
- Protein: ~15g
- Carbohydrates: ~35g
- Fiber: ~10g
- Fat: ~7g

CAULIFLOWER AND WHITE BEAN TACOS

Ingredients:

- 2 cups cauliflower florets
- 1 can (15 oz) white beans, drained and rinsed
- 1 teaspoon chilli powder
- 1/2 teaspoon cumin
- 1/2 teaspoon paprika
- Salt and pepper to taste
- 8 small corn or whole wheat tortillas
- Toppings: diced tomatoes, shredded lettuce, diced red onion, chopped cilantro, lime wedges

Instructions:

1. Turn the oven on and set it to 400°F (200°C).
2. Add olive oil, chilli powder, cumin, paprika, salt, and pepper to the cauliflower pieces.
3. Spread the cauliflower on a baking sheet and roast it for about 20 to 25 minutes until it is soft but still has a little crunch.
4. Mash the white beans in a bowl with a fork or a potato masher until they are chunky.
5. Follow the directions on the package to heat the tortillas.
6. Put the tacos together by putting mashed white beans on each tortilla, then adding roasted cauliflower and any other toppings you want.
7. Serve the tacos with broccoli and white beans with wedges of lime.

Nutrition (per serving, 2 tacos):

- Calories: ~250

- Protein: ~10g
- Carbohydrates: ~45g
- Fiber: ~10g
- Fat: ~4g

LENTIL AND VEGETABLE COCONUT CURRY

Ingredients:

- 1 cup green or brown lentils, uncooked
- 1 tablespoon coconut oil
- 1 onion, chopped
- 2 carrots, peeled and diced
- 1 bell pepper, diced
- 1 zucchini, diced
- 3 cloves garlic, minced
- 1 tablespoon curry powder
- 1 teaspoon ground turmeric
- 1/2 teaspoon ground cumin
- 1/2 teaspoon ground coriander
- 1 can (14 oz) coconut milk
- 2 cups vegetable broth
- Juice of 1 lime
- Salt and pepper to taste
- Fresh cilantro for garnish
- Cooked rice for serving

Instructions:

1. Rinse the lentils with cold water and put them to the side.

2. Over medium heat, melt the coconut oil in a big pot. Add the chopped onion, carrots, bell pepper, and zucchini. Sauté the veggies for about 5–7 minutes or until they get soft.
3. Mix in the chopped garlic, curry powder, turmeric powder, cumin powder, and coriander powder. Cook for another 1–2 minutes until the food smells good.
4. Add the lentils that have been rinsed, the coconut milk, and the veggie broth.
5. Bring the mixture to a boil, turn the heat down to low, cover, and let the curry cook for about 20 to 25 minutes, or until the lentils are soft.
6. Squeeze the lime juice into the dish and season to taste with salt and pepper.
7. Serve the lentil and veggie soup with cooked rice and fresh cilantro.

Nutrition (per serving):
- Calories: ~300
- Protein: ~15g
- Carbohydrates: ~45g
- Fiber: ~12g
- Fat: ~10g

HIGH-FIBER BANANA WALNUT MUFFINS

Ingredients:
- 1 1/2 cups whole wheat flour
- 1/2 cup rolled oats

- 1/4 cup ground flaxseed
- 1 teaspoon baking soda
- 1/2 teaspoon baking powder
- 1/2 teaspoon cinnamon
- 1/4 teaspoon salt
- 3 ripe bananas, mashed
- 1/2 cup Greek yogurt
- 1/4 cup honey or maple syrup
- 1 large egg
- 1 teaspoon vanilla extract
- 1/2 cup chopped walnuts

Instructions:

1. Turn the oven on and set it to 350°F (175°C). Use paper cups to line a muffin pan.
2. Mix the whole wheat flour, rolled oats, ground flaxseed, baking soda, baking powder, cinnamon, and salt in a big bowl with a whisk.
3. Mix the mashed bananas, Greek yoghurt, honey or maple syrup, egg, and vanilla extract in another bowl until everything is well mixed.
4. Pour the wet ingredients into the dry ingredients and stir until just mixed. Don't mix too much.
5. Mix in the chopped walnuts with care.
6. Put the same amount of batter in each muffin cup.
7. Bake in an oven that has already been heated for about 18 to 20 minutes or until a knife stuck into the middle of a muffin comes out clean.
8. Let the muffins cool for a few minutes in the pan before moving them to a wire rack to finish cooling.

Nutrition (per muffin):

- Calories: ~200

- Protein: ~5g
- Carbohydrates: ~30g
- Fiber: ~5g
- Fat: ~7g

MEXICAN QUINOA STUFFED PEPPERS

Ingredients:

- 4 large bell peppers, any colour
- 1 cup quinoa, rinsed
- 2 cups vegetable broth
- 1 can (15 oz) black beans, drained and rinsed
- 1 cup corn kernels (fresh, frozen, or canned)
- 1 cup diced tomatoes
- 1 teaspoon chilli powder
- 1/2 teaspoon cumin
- 1/4 teaspoon paprika
- Salt and pepper to taste
- 1 cup shredded cheddar cheese
- Fresh cilantro for garnish

Instructions:

1. Turn the oven on and set it to 375°F (190°C).
2. Remove the seeds and skins from the bell peppers and cut off the tops.
3. Mix the quinoa and veggie broth in a medium saucepan. Bring to a boil, then boil the heat to low, cover, and simmer for 15 to 20 minutes, or until the quinoa is cooked and the liquid is absorbed.

4. Mix the cooked quinoa, black beans, corn kernels, diced tomatoes, chilli powder, cumin, paprika, salt, and pepper in a big bowl.
5. Put the rice mixture into the bell peppers that have been cut open.
6. Put the peppers in an oven dish and cover them with aluminium foil.
7. Bake for about 25 to 30 minutes in an oven that has already been warm or until the peppers are soft.
8. Take off the paper, sprinkle each pepper with shredded cheddar cheese, and put them back in the oven for a few minutes or until the cheese is melted and bubbly.
9. Before serving, sprinkle fresh cilantro on top.

Nutrition (per serving, one stuffed pepper):

- Calories: ~350
- Protein: ~15g
- Carbohydrates: ~55g
- Fiber: ~12g
- Fat: ~10g

SPAGHETTI SQUASH WITH CHICKPEA MARINARA

Ingredients:

- 1 medium spaghetti squash
- 1 can (15 oz) chickpeas, drained and rinsed
- 2 cups diced tomatoes (canned or fresh)
- 1/2 cup diced onion
- 2 cloves garlic, minced

- 1 teaspoon dried basil
- 1/2 teaspoon dried oregano
- 1/4 teaspoon red pepper flakes (optional)
- Salt and pepper to taste
- Olive oil for drizzling
- Fresh basil leaves for garnish
- Grated Parmesan cheese for serving

Instructions:

1. Turn the oven on and set it to 400°F (200°C).
2. Split the spaghetti squash in half lengthwise and scoop out the seeds.
3. Cut side up and put the spaghetti squash halves on a baking sheet. Add some olive oil and salt and pepper to taste.
4. When the oven is hot, roast the spaghetti squash for about 40 to 45 minutes or until the flesh can be easily scraped into strands with a fork.
5. Heat olive oil in a pan over medium heat. Add the chopped onion and cook for about 3 to 4 minutes until the onion becomes clear.
6. Add the chopped garlic and cook for another minute or until the garlic smells good.
7. Mix in the diced tomatoes, dried basil, dried oregano, red pepper flakes (if using), salt, and pepper. Cook the chickpeas for 10 to 15 minutes to make the tomato sauce.
8. Add the beans to the marinara sauce and cook for 5–7 minutes.
9. Once the spaghetti squash has been roasted, you can use a fork to pull out the spaghetti-like strands of meat.
10. Serve the chickpea marinara sauce on top of the spaghetti squash.

11. Sprinkle chopped Parmesan cheese and fresh basil leaves on top.

Nutrition (per serving):

- Calories: ~300
- Protein: ~10g
- Carbohydrates: ~50g
- Fiber: ~10g
- Fat: ~8g

THREE-BEAN AND FARRO SALAD

Ingredients:

- 1 cup farro, rinsed
- 2 1/2 cups water or vegetable broth
- 1 can (15 oz) kidney beans, drained and rinsed
- 1 can (15 oz) black beans, drained and rinsed
- 1 can (15 oz) chickpeas, drained and rinsed
- 1 cup diced cucumber
- 1 cup diced bell peppers (any colour)
- 1/2 cup diced red onion
- 1/4 cup chopped fresh parsley
- 1/4 cup chopped fresh cilantro
- Juice of 1 lemon
- 3 tablespoons extra-virgin olive oil
- Salt and pepper to taste

Instructions:

1. Mix the farro and water or veggie broth in a medium saucepan. Bring to a boil, boil the heat to low, cover, and

simmer for 25 to 30 minutes or until the farro is soft. Pour out any extra liquid.

2. Cooked farro, kidney beans, black beans, chickpeas, diced cucumber, bell peppers, red onion, chopped parsley, and chopped cilantro are all mixed together in a big bowl.
3. Mix the lemon juice, extra-virgin olive oil, salt, and pepper in a small bowl with a whisk to make the sauce.
4. Pour the sauce over the salad and mix it well.
5. The three-bean and farro salad is a filling and healthy dish to serve.

Nutrition (per serving):

- Calories: ~350
- Protein: ~15g
- Carbohydrates: ~60g
- Fiber: ~15g
- Fat: ~8g

ROASTED VEGETABLE AND AVOCADO WRAP

Ingredients:

- 1 cup mixed roasted vegetables (such as bell peppers, zucchini, eggplant, and onion)
- 1 avocado, sliced
- 2 whole wheat tortillas
- 1/4 cup hummus
- 1/4 cup crumbled feta cheese
- Fresh spinach leaves
- Salt and pepper to taste

Instructions:

1. Follow the directions on the package to heat the whole wheat tortillas.
2. Each tortilla should have 2 tablespoons of hummus on it.
3. On top of the hummus, put the fresh spinach leaves.
4. Mix the roasted veggies and put them on each tortilla.
5. Sliced avocado and chopped feta cheese should go on top.
6. Salt and pepper can be added to taste.
7. To make wraps, tightly roll the tortillas.

Nutrition (per wrap):

- Calories: ~350
- Protein: ~10g
- Carbohydrates: ~40g
- Fiber: ~10g
- Fat: ~18g

FIBER-PACKED APPLE CINNAMON WAFFLES

Ingredients:

- 1 cup whole wheat flour
- 1/2 cup oat flour (ground oats)
- 1/4 cup ground flaxseed
- 1 tablespoon baking powder
- 1 teaspoon ground cinnamon
- 1/4 teaspoon salt
- 1 cup almond milk (or any milk of choice)
- 1/4 cup unsweetened applesauce
- 2 tablespoons melted coconut oil or butter

- 1 tablespoon honey or maple syrup
- 1 teaspoon vanilla extract
- 1 apple, peeled and grated

Instructions:

1. Follow the guidelines that came with the waffle iron to heat it.
2. Whisk the whole wheat flour, oat flour, ground flaxseed, baking powder, ground cinnamon, and salt in a big bowl.
3. Combine the almond milk, applesauce, honey or maple syrup, melted coconut oil or butter, and vanilla extract in another bowl.
4. Pour the wet ingredients into the dry ingredients and stir until just mixed.
5. Gently add the chopped apple.
6. Use a little oil or nonstick spray to grease the waffle pan.
7. Pour the waffle batter onto the waffle iron that has already been heated up, as the maker directs.
8. Cook the waffles until they are crisp and golden brown.
9. Apple cinnamon waffles are full of fibre and can be topped with anything you like.

Nutrition (per waffle, recipe makes about four waffles):

- Calories: ~250
- Protein: ~8g
- Carbohydrates: ~35g
- Fiber: ~8g
- Fat: ~10g

THAI RED CURRY LENTIL SOUP

Ingredients:

- 1 cup green or brown lentils, uncooked
- 1 tablespoon coconut oil
- 1 onion, chopped
- 2 carrots, peeled and diced
- 1 bell pepper, diced
- 3 cloves garlic, minced
- 2 tablespoons Thai red curry paste
- 1 can (14 oz) coconut milk
- 4 cups vegetable broth
- 1 tablespoon soy sauce
- Juice of 1 lime
- Salt and pepper to taste
- Fresh cilantro and lime wedges for garnish

Instructions:

1. Rinse the lentils with cold water and put them to the side.
2. Over medium heat, melt the coconut oil in a big pot. Add the chopped onion, chopped carrots, and chopped bell pepper. Sauté the veggies for about 5–7 minutes or until they get soft.
3. Mix in the chopped garlic and Thai red curry paste. Cook for another 1–2 minutes until the food smells good.
4. Add the lentils that have been rinsed, the coconut milk, the veggie broth, and the soy sauce.
5. Bring the soup to a boil, turn the heat down to low, cover, and cook for about 20 to 25 minutes or until the lentils are soft.
6. Squeeze the lime juice into the dish and season to taste with salt and pepper.
7. Add fresh cilantro and lime wedges to the Thai red curry lentil soup as a topping.

Nutrition (per serving):

- Calories: ~300
- Protein: ~15g
- Carbohydrates: ~40g
- Fiber: ~12g
- Fat: ~10g

STUFFED ZUCCHINI WITH QUINOA AND PESTO

Ingredients:

- 4 medium zucchini
- 1 cup cooked quinoa
- 1/2 cup cherry tomatoes, halved
- 1/4 cup crumbled feta cheese
- 1/4 cup prepared pesto
- Salt and pepper to taste
- Olive oil for drizzling
- Fresh basil leaves for garnish

Instructions:

1. Turn the oven on and set it to 375°F (190°C).
2. Cut the zucchini in half lengthwise and scoop out the middle to make zucchini boats.
3. In a bowl, mix the cooked quinoa, cherry tomatoes cut in half, chopped feta cheese, and pesto that has already been made.
4. Add salt and pepper to taste to the mixture.
5. Put the rice mixture into the zucchini boats.

6. Put the stuffed zucchini on a baking sheet and drizzle with olive oil.
7. Bake in an oven that has already been warm for 20 to 25 minutes or until the zucchini is soft and the filling is hot.
8. Before serving, top with fresh basil leaves.

Nutrition (per serving, 2 stuffed zucchini halves):

- Calories: ~300
- Protein: ~10g
- Carbohydrates: ~35g
- Fiber: ~6g
- Fat: ~15g

MANGO AND CHIA SEED SMOOTHIE

Ingredients:

- 1 ripe mango, peeled and pitted
- 1 banana
- 1 cup almond milk (or any milk of choice)
- 2 tablespoons chia seeds
- 1 tablespoon honey or maple syrup
- Ice cubes

Instructions:

1. Mix the ripe mango, banana, almond milk, chia seeds, honey or maple syrup, and ice cubes in a blender.
2. Blend until smooth and creamy. If you need to, add more milk to get the right consistency.
3. Taste it and add or take away sugar as needed.
4. Pour the smoothie made with mango and chia seeds into cups and drink it immediately.

Nutrition (per serving):

- Calories: ~250
- Protein: ~5g
- Carbohydrates: ~45g
- Fiber: ~8g
- Fat: ~7g

ROASTED BRUSSELS SPROUTS AND QUINOA BOWL

Ingredients:

- 2 cups Brussels sprouts, trimmed and halved
- 1 tablespoon olive oil
- Salt and pepper to taste
- 1 cup cooked quinoa
- 1/2 cup cooked chickpeas
- 1/4 cup dried cranberries
- 1/4 cup chopped walnuts
- Balsamic vinegar for drizzling

Instructions:

1. Turn the oven on and set it to 400°F (200°C).
2. Mix the olive oil, salt, and pepper with the split Brussels sprouts.
3. Spread the Brussels sprouts on a baking sheet and roast them for about 20 to 25 minutes until golden and crispy.
4. Put the quinoa, roasted Brussels sprouts, cooked chickpeas, dried cranberries, and chopped walnuts into bowls for serving.
5. To serve, drizzle with balsamic vinegar.

Nutrition (per serving):

- Calories: ~350
- Protein: ~10g
- Carbohydrates: ~45g
- Fiber: ~10g
- Fat: ~15g

HIGH-FIBER GREEK VEGGIE SANDWICH

Ingredients:

- 2 slices whole grain bread
- 1/4 cup hummus
- 1/4 cup crumbled feta cheese
- 1/2 cup sliced cucumber
- 1/2 cup sliced bell peppers (any colour)
- 1/4 cup sliced red onion
- 1/4 cup sliced Kalamata olives
- 1/4 cup mixed greens or arugula
- Olive oil and red wine vinegar for drizzling
- Salt and pepper to taste

Instructions:

1. On one side of each piece of bread, spread hummus.
2. Put crumbled feta cheese, sliced cucumber, bell peppers, red onion, Kalamata olives, and lettuce or mixed greens on one slice of bread.
3. Olive oil and red wine vinegar should be poured over the vegetables.
4. Salt and pepper can be added to taste.

5. Add the other slice of bread on top to make a sandwich.

Nutrition (per sandwich):

- Calories: ~350
- Protein: ~10g
- Carbohydrates: ~40g
- Fiber: ~8g
- Fat: ~15g

BLACK BEAN AND SWEET POTATO TACOS

Ingredients:

- 1 large sweet potato, peeled and diced
- 1 tablespoon olive oil
- 1 teaspoon chilli powder
- 1/2 teaspoon cumin
- 1/4 teaspoon paprika
- Salt and pepper to taste
- 1 can (15 oz) black beans, drained and rinsed
- 8 small corn or whole wheat tortillas
- Toppings: diced avocado, chopped fresh cilantro, lime wedges

Instructions:

1. Turn the oven on and set it to 400°F (200°C).
2. Mix the diced sweet potatoes with olive oil, chilli powder, cumin, paprika, salt, and pepper.

3. Spread the sweet potato on a baking sheet and roast it for about 20 to 25 minutes, or until it is soft but still has a little crunch.
4. With a fork or a potato masher, mash the black beans in a bowl until they are chunky.
5. Follow the directions on the package to heat the tortillas.
6. Put the tacos together by putting mashed black beans on each tortilla, then adding roasted sweet potato and any other toppings you like.
7. Serve the sweet potato and black bean tacos with pieces of lime.

Nutrition (per serving, two tacos):

- Calories: ~300
- Protein: ~10g
- Carbohydrates: ~50g
- Fiber: ~12g
- Fat: ~6g

FIBER-RICH PUMPKIN SPICE PANCAKES

Ingredients:

- 1 cup whole wheat flour
- 1/4 cup ground flaxseed
- 1 teaspoon baking powder
- 1/2 teaspoon baking soda
- 1 teaspoon ground cinnamon
- 1/2 teaspoon ground nutmeg
- 1/4 teaspoon ground ginger

- 1/4 teaspoon ground cloves
- 1/4 teaspoon salt
- 1/2 cup pumpkin puree
- 1 cup buttermilk (or milk of choice)
- 1 large egg
- 2 tablespoons honey or maple syrup
- 1 teaspoon vanilla extract

Instructions:

1. Mix the whole wheat flour, ground flaxseed, baking powder, baking soda, cinnamon, nutmeg, ginger, cloves, and salt in a big bowl with a whisk.
2. Mix the pumpkin puree, buttermilk, egg, honey or maple syrup, and vanilla extract in another bowl until they are well blended.
3. Pour the wet ingredients into the dry ingredients and stir until just mixed. Don't mix the batter too much; a few lumps are fine.
4. Heat a pan or grill over medium heat and lightly grease it with butter or oil.
5. For each pancake, pour 1/4 cup of batter into the pan.
6. Cook the pancake until bubbles appear on the top, then flip it and cook for another 1–2 minutes until golden brown.
7. Pumpkin spice pancakes are full of fibre and can be topped with anything you like.

Nutrition (per pancake, recipe makes about eight pancakes):

- Calories: ~150
- Protein: ~5g
- Carbohydrates: ~25g
- Fiber: ~5g

- Fat: ~3g

MEDITERRANEAN LENTIL AND VEGETABLE STIR-FRY

Ingredients:

- 1 cup cooked green or brown lentils
- 1 cup diced eggplant
- 1 cup diced zucchini
- 1 cup cherry tomatoes, halved
- 1/2 cup diced red onion
- 2 cloves garlic, minced
- 1 teaspoon dried oregano
- 1/2 teaspoon dried basil
- Salt and pepper to taste
- 2 tablespoons olive oil
- Juice of 1 lemon
- Fresh parsley for garnish

Instructions:

1. Olive oil is heated over medium heat in a large pot.
2. Add cut pieces of eggplant, zucchini, red onion, and minced garlic. Sauté the veggies for about 5 to 7 minutes or until they get soft.
3. Mix in the cooked lentils, cherry tomatoes cut in half, dried oregano, dried basil, salt, and pepper. Cook for another 3–4 minutes to heat it through.
4. Squeeze the lemon juice in and mix everything.
5. Add some fresh parsley as a garnish before serving.

Nutrition (per serving):

- Calories: ~250
- Protein: ~10g
- Carbohydrates: ~35g
- Fiber: ~10g
- Fat: ~8g

QUINOA AND BLACK BEAN STUFFED BELL PEPPERS

Ingredients:

- 4 large bell peppers, any colour
- 1 cup cooked quinoa
- 1 can (15 oz) black beans, drained and rinsed
- 1 cup corn kernels (fresh, frozen, or canned)
- 1 cup diced tomatoes
- 1 teaspoon chilli powder
- 1/2 teaspoon cumin
- 1/4 teaspoon paprika
- Salt and pepper to taste
- 1 cup shredded cheddar cheese

Instructions:

1. Turn the oven on and set it to 375°F (190°C).
2. Remove the seeds and skins from the bell peppers and cut off the tops.
3. Cooked rice, black beans, corn kernels, diced tomatoes, chilli powder, cumin, paprika, salt, and pepper are all mixed in a bowl.

4. Put the rice mixture into the bell peppers that have been cut open.
5. Put the peppers in an oven dish and cover them with aluminium foil.
6. Bake for about 25 to 30 minutes in an oven that has already been warm or until the peppers are soft.
7. Take off the paper, sprinkle each pepper with shredded cheddar cheese, and put them back in the oven for a few minutes or until the cheese is melted and bubbly.
8. Serve the bell peppers stuffed with rice and black beans.

Nutrition (per serving, one stuffed pepper):
- Calories: ~350
- Protein: ~15g
- Carbohydrates: ~50g
- Fiber: ~12g
- Fat: ~10g

MIXED BERRY CHIA SEED OATMEAL

Ingredients:
- 1/2 cup rolled oats
- 1 cup almond milk (or any milk of choice)
- 1/2 cup mixed berries (blueberries, raspberries, strawberries)
- 1 tablespoon chia seeds
- 1 tablespoon honey or maple syrup
- Chopped nuts for topping (optional)

Instructions:

1. Mix the rolled oats and almond milk in a pot.
2. Cook over medium heat, stirring occasionally, for about 5 to 7 minutes or until the oats are done and the sauce has thickened.
3. Take it off the heat and add the mixed berries and chia seeds.
4. Honey or maple syrup can be added to taste.
5. If you want, you can serve the mixed berry chia seed oatmeal with chopped nuts on top.

Nutrition (per serving):

- Calories: ~250
- Protein: ~6g
- Carbohydrates: ~40g
- Fiber: ~8g
- Fat: ~7g

SWEET POTATO AND LENTIL TACOS

Ingredients:

- 2 cups cooked and mashed sweet potatoes
- 1 cup cooked green or brown lentils
- 1 teaspoon chilli powder
- 1/2 teaspoon ground cumin
- 1/4 teaspoon smoked paprika
- Salt and pepper to taste
- 8 small corn or whole wheat tortillas
- Toppings: diced avocado, chopped fresh cilantro, lime wedges

Instructions:

1. Mix the mashed sweet potatoes and cooked lentils together in a bowl.
2. Mix in the salt, pepper, chilli powder, ground cumin, smoked paprika, and smoked paprika.
3. Follow the directions on the package to heat the tortillas.
4. Spread sweet potato and lentil filling on each tortilla to make a taco.
5. Add toppings like diced avocado and chopped fresh parsley if you want.
6. Sweet potato and bean tacos should be served with lime wedges.

Nutrition (per serving, two tacos):

- Calories: ~300
- Protein: ~10g
- Carbohydrates: ~50g
- Fiber: ~12g
- Fat: ~4g

WHOLE WHEAT VEGGIE FRITTATA

Ingredients:

- 6 large eggs
- 1/2 cup diced bell peppers (any colour)
- 1/2 cup diced zucchini
- 1/4 cup diced red onion
- 1/4 cup chopped spinach or kale
- 1/4 cup crumbled feta cheese
- 2 tablespoons chopped fresh parsley

- Salt and pepper to taste
- Olive oil for cooking

Instructions:

1. Set the oven temperature to 375°F (190°C).
2. Whisk the eggs in a bowl until they are well beaten.
3. Pour a little olive oil into a pan that can go from stovetop to oven and heat it over medium heat.
4. Add bell peppers, zucchini, and red onion that have been cut into small pieces. Sauté the veggies for about 5–7 minutes or until they soften.
5. Stir in the chopped spinach or kale and cook for another 1–2 minutes, until the greens have softened.
6. Pour the beaten eggs over the veggies that have been sautéed.
7. On top of the eggs, sprinkle broken feta cheese and chopped fresh parsley.
8. Let the frittata cook on the stove for a few minutes until the edges start to set.
9. Place the pan in a preheated oven and bake for about 12 to 15 minutes, or until the top of the frittata is set and a little golden.
10. Take the whole wheat veggie frittata out of the oven, cut it into pieces, and serve.

Nutrition (per serving):

- Calories: ~200
- Protein: ~12g
- Carbohydrates: ~10g
- Fiber: ~2g
- Fat: ~12g

FIBER-PACKED GREEN GODDESS SMOOTHIE

Ingredients:

- 1 cup spinach leaves
- 1/2 cup kale leaves, stems removed
- 1/2 avocado
- 1 banana
- 1 tablespoon chia seeds
- 1 cup almond milk (or any milk of choice)
- 1/2 cup Greek yoghurt (plain or vanilla)
- Honey or maple syrup to taste (optional)

Instructions:

1. Put spinach, kale, avocado, banana, chia seeds, almond milk, and Greek yoghurt in a blender.
2. Mix until creamy and smooth.
3. If you want, you can add honey or maple syrup to sweeten it.
4. Pour the green goddess juice, which is full of fibre, into glasses and enjoy.

Nutrition (per serving):

- Calories: ~250
- Protein: ~10g
- Carbohydrates: ~35g
- Fiber: ~10g
- Fat: ~10g

ROASTED VEGETABLE AND HUMMUS PANINI

Ingredients:

- 8 slices whole grain bread
- 1 cup mixed roasted vegetables (such as bell peppers, zucchini, eggplant, and onion)
- 1/2 cup hummus
- 1/2 cup baby spinach leaves
- Olive oil for brushing

Instructions:

1. Heat a sandwich press or a grill pan on the stove.
2. Each piece of bread should have 1 tablespoon of hummus on it.
3. Stack baby spinach leaves and roasted mixed veggies on top of one slice of bread.
4. Make a sandwich by putting another slice of bread on top.
5. Brush a little olive oil on the outside of the sandwich.
6. Grill the sandwich until the bread is toasted and crispy and the filling is hot all the way through.
7. Cut the roasted veggie and hummus panini in half and put it on a plate.

Nutrition (per panini):

- Calories: ~300
- Protein: ~10g
- Carbohydrates: ~45g
- Fiber: ~8g
- Fat: ~10g

RED LENTIL AND SWEET POTATO CURRY

Ingredients:

- 1 cup red lentils, uncooked
- 2 cups diced sweet potatoes
- 1 onion, chopped
- 2 cloves garlic, minced
- 1 tablespoon curry powder
- 1 teaspoon ground turmeric
- 1/2 teaspoon ground cumin
- 1/4 teaspoon cayenne pepper (adjust to taste)
- 1 can (14 oz) coconut milk
- 2 cups vegetable broth
- Juice of 1 lemon
- Salt and pepper to taste
- Fresh cilantro for garnish
- Cooked rice for serving

Instructions:

1. Rinse the red lentils under cold water and set them away.
2. In a big pot, sauté the chopped onion in olive oil until it turns clear.
3. Mix in the chopped garlic, curry powder, turmeric powder, cumin powder, and cayenne pepper. Cook for another 1–2 minutes until the food smells good.
4. Mix in the chopped sweet potatoes and cleaned red lentils.
5. Add the coconut milk and the veggie broth. Bring the mixture to a boil, turn the heat down to low, cover, and cook for about 20 to 25 minutes, or until the lentils and sweet potatoes are soft.

6. Squeeze the lemon juice into the dish and season to taste with salt and pepper.
7. Red lentil and sweet potato soup go well with cooked rice and fresh cilantro.

Nutrition (per serving):

- Calories: ~350
- Protein: ~15g
- Carbohydrates: ~50g
- Fiber: ~12g
- Fat: ~10g

HIGH-FIBER CHOCOLATE BANANA MUFFINS

Ingredients:

- 1 1/2 cups whole wheat flour
- 1/4 cup cocoa powder
- 1/4 cup ground flaxseed
- 1 teaspoon baking powder
- 1/2 teaspoon baking soda
- 1/2 teaspoon ground cinnamon
- 1/4 teaspoon salt
- 3 ripe bananas, mashed
- 1/2 cup Greek yogurt
- 1/4 cup honey or maple syrup
- 1 large egg
- 1 teaspoon vanilla extract
- 1/4 cup dark chocolate chips

Instructions:

1. Turn the oven on and set it to 350°F (175°C). Use paper cups to line a muffin pan.
2. Mix the whole wheat flour, cocoa powder, ground flaxseed, baking powder, baking soda, ground cinnamon, and salt in a big bowl with a whisk.
3. Mix the mashed bananas, Greek yoghurt, honey or maple syrup, egg, and vanilla extract in another bowl.
4. Pour the wet ingredients into the dry ingredients and stir until just mixed.
5. Gently add the dark chocolate chips.
6. Put the same amount of batter in each muffin cup.
7. Bake in an oven that has already been heated for about 18 to 20 minutes or until a knife stuck into the middle of a muffin comes out clean.
8. Let the muffins cool for a few minutes in the pan before moving them to a wire rack to finish cooling.

Nutrition (per muffin, recipe makes about 12 muffins):

- Calories: ~150
- Protein: ~4g
- Carbohydrates: ~30g
- Fiber: ~5g
- Fat: ~3g

CAPRESE QUINOA STUFFED TOMATOES

Ingredients:

- 4 large tomatoes

- 1 cup cooked quinoa
- 1/2 cup fresh mozzarella balls, halved
- 1/4 cup chopped fresh basil
- 2 tablespoons balsamic vinegar
- 2 tablespoons olive oil
- Salt and pepper to taste

Instructions:

1. To make tomato cups, cut off the tops of the tomatoes and scoop out the pulp and seeds.
2. Mix the cooked rice, fresh mozzarella balls, fresh basil that has been chopped, balsamic vinegar, olive oil, salt, and pepper in a bowl.
3. Put the rice mixture into the tomatoes that have been cut open.
4. The quinoa-stuffed caprese tomatoes are a light and tasty dish.

Nutrition (per serving, 1 stuffed tomato):

- Calories: ~250
- Protein: ~8g
- Carbohydrates: ~20g
- Fiber: ~4g
- Fat: ~15g

CHICKPEA AND SPINACH BREAKFAST BURRITO

Ingredients:

- 1 cup cooked chickpeas

- 2 cups baby spinach leaves
- 4 large eggs
- 4 whole wheat tortillas
- 1/4 cup crumbled feta cheese
- Salt and pepper to taste
- Olive oil for cooking

Instructions:

1. Heat a little olive oil in a pan over medium heat.
2. Add chickpeas that have been cooked and baby spinach leaves. Sauté for about 3–4 minutes until the spinach wilts and the chickpeas are hot.
3. Whisk the eggs in a bowl and add salt and pepper.
4. Move the beans and spinach to one side of the pan and pour the whisked eggs into the other.
5. Scramble the eggs until they are fully cooked.
6. The whole wheat tortillas can be heated in a pan or in the microwave.
7. Put the morning burritos together by putting some chickpea, spinach mixture, and scrambled eggs on each tortilla.
8. Crumble some feta cheese on top, and roll the dough to make burritos.

Nutrition (per burrito):

- Calories: ~350
- Protein: ~15g
- Carbohydrates: ~40g
- Fiber: ~10g
- Fat: ~15g

SPAGHETTI SQUASH WITH LENTIL BOLOGNESE

Ingredients:

- 1 medium spaghetti squash
- 1 cup green or brown lentils, uncooked
- 1 can (14 oz) crushed tomatoes
- 1 onion, chopped
- 2 cloves garlic, minced
- 1 teaspoon dried basil
- 1/2 teaspoon dried oregano
- 1/4 teaspoon red pepper flakes (optional)
- Salt and pepper to taste
- Olive oil for cooking
- Fresh parsley for garnish

Instructions:

1. Turn the oven on and set it to 400°F (200°C).
2. Split the spaghetti squash in half lengthwise and scoop out the seeds.
3. Cut side up and put the spaghetti squash halves on a baking sheet. Add some olive oil and salt and pepper to taste.
4. When the oven is hot, roast the spaghetti squash for about 40 to 45 minutes or until the flesh can be easily scraped into strands with a fork.
5. Rinse the lentils with cold water and put them to the side.
6. Heat olive oil in a pan over medium heat. Add the chopped onion and cook for about 3 to 4 minutes until the onion becomes clear.
7. Add the minced garlic and cook for another minute or until the garlic smells good.

8. Mix in the crushed tomatoes, dried basil, dried oregano, red pepper flakes (if using), salt, and pepper. To make the lentil bolognese sauce, cook the lentils for about 10 to 15 minutes.
9. Stir the beans into the sauce to mix everything. Continue cooking for another 20 to 25 minutes or until the lentils are soft.
10. Once the spaghetti squash has been roasted, you can use a fork to pull out the spaghetti-like strands of meat.
11. Serve the lentil bolognese sauce on top of the spaghetti squash.
12. Add some fresh parsley as a garnish before serving.

Nutrition (per serving):

- Calories: ~300
- Protein: ~15g
- Carbohydrates: ~50g
- Fiber: ~15g
- Fat: ~5g

THREE-BEAN AND BARLEY SALAD

Ingredients:

- 1 cup cooked barley
- 1 can (15 oz) kidney beans, drained and rinsed
- 1 can (15 oz) black beans, drained and rinsed
- 1 can (15 oz) chickpeas, drained and rinsed
- 1 cup diced cucumber
- 1/2 cup diced bell peppers (any colour)
- 1/4 cup diced red onion

- 1/4 cup chopped fresh parsley
- 1/4 cup chopped fresh cilantro
- Juice of 1 lemon
- 3 tablespoons extra-virgin olive oil
- Salt and pepper to taste

Instructions:

1. Cooked barley, kidney beans, black beans, chickpeas, diced cucumber, bell peppers, red onion, chopped parsley, and chopped cilantro are all mixed together in a big bowl.
2. Mix the lemon juice, extra-virgin olive oil, salt, and pepper in a small bowl with a whisk to make the sauce.
3. Pour the sauce over the salad and mix it well.
4. A filling and healthy dish is the three-bean and barley salad.

Nutrition (per serving):

- Calories: ~350
- Protein: ~15g
- Carbohydrates: ~60g
- Fiber: ~15g
- Fat: ~8g

ROASTED RED PEPPER AND AVOCADO WRAP

Ingredients:

- 2 large whole wheat tortillas

- 1 cup roasted red peppers, sliced
- 1 avocado, sliced
- 1/4 cup hummus
- 1/4 cup crumbled feta cheese
- Fresh spinach leaves
- Salt and pepper to taste

Instructions:

1. Follow the directions on the package to heat the whole wheat tortillas.
2. Each tortilla should have 2 tablespoons of hummus on it.
3. On top of the hummus, lay down raw spinach leaves.
4. Split the pieces of roasted red pepper and avocado between the tortillas.
5. Crumble some feta cheese on top.
6. Salt and pepper can be added to taste.
7. To make wraps, tightly roll the tortillas.

Nutrition (per wrap):

- Calories: ~350
- Protein: ~10g
- Carbohydrates: ~40g
- Fiber: ~10g
- Fat: ~18g

FIBER-RICH BLUEBERRY BANANA OATMEAL

Ingredients:

- 1/2 cup rolled oats

- 1 cup almond milk (or any milk of choice)
- 1/2 cup fresh blueberries
- 1 banana, sliced
- 1 tablespoon chia seeds
- 1 tablespoon ground flaxseed
- 1 tablespoon honey or maple syrup
- Chopped nuts for topping (optional)

Instructions:

1. Mix the rolled oats and almond milk in a pot.
2. Cook over medium heat, stirring occasionally, for about 5 to 7 minutes or until the oats are done and the sauce has thickened.
3. Stir in the fresh blueberries, sliced bananas, chia seeds, and flaxseed meal.
4. Honey or maple syrup can be added to taste.
5. If you want, you can top the high-fibre blueberry banana cereal with chopped nuts.

Nutrition (per serving):

- Calories: ~300
- Protein: ~7g
- Carbohydrates: ~50g
- Fiber: ~10g
- Fat: ~8g

CURRIED LENTIL AND VEGETABLE STEW

Ingredients:

- 1 cup green or brown lentils, uncooked
- 2 cups diced carrots
- 2 cups diced potatoes
- 1 onion, chopped
- 2 cloves garlic, minced
- 1 tablespoon curry powder
- 1/2 teaspoon ground turmeric
- 1/2 teaspoon ground cumin
- 1/4 teaspoon cayenne pepper (adjust to taste)
- Salt and pepper to taste
- 4 cups vegetable broth
- 1 can (14 oz) coconut milk
- Fresh cilantro for garnish

Instructions:

1. Rinse the lentils with cold water and put them to the side.
2. In a big pot, sauté the chopped onion in olive oil until it turns clear.
3. Add carrots and potatoes cut into small pieces. Sauté the veggies for about 5 to 7 minutes or until they get soft.
4. Mix in the chopped garlic, curry powder, turmeric powder, cumin powder, cayenne pepper, salt, and pepper. Cook for another 1–2 minutes until the food smells good.
5. Add the lentils that have been rinsed, the veggie broth, and the coconut milk.
6. Bring the stew to a boil, then turn the heat down to low, cover, and let it simmer for about 20 to 25 minutes, or until the lentils and veggies are soft.
7. Taste it and, if necessary, change the flavour.
8. Serve the lentil and veggie stew with a fresh sprig of cilantro on top.

Nutrition (per serving):

- Calories: ~350
- Protein: ~15g
- Carbohydrates: ~50g
- Fiber: ~15g
- Fat: ~10g

STUFFED BELL PEPPERS WITH QUINOA AND FETA

Ingredients:

- 4 large bell peppers, any colour
- 1 cup cooked quinoa
- 1/2 cup crumbled feta cheese
- 1/4 cup diced red onion
- 1/4 cup chopped fresh parsley
- 1/4 cup chopped fresh mint
- 1/4 cup chopped walnuts
- 2 tablespoons olive oil
- Juice of 1 lemon
- Salt and pepper to taste

Instructions:

1. Turn the oven on and set it to 375°F (190°C).
2. Remove the seeds and skins from the bell peppers and cut off the tops.
3. Mix the cooked quinoa, crumbled feta cheese, diced red onion, chopped fresh parsley, chopped fresh mint, chopped walnuts, olive oil, lemon juice, salt, and pepper in a bowl.

4. Put the rice mixture into the bell peppers that have been cut open.
5. Put the peppers in an oven dish and cover them with aluminium foil.
6. Bake for about 25 to 30 minutes in an oven that has already been warm or until the peppers are soft.
7. As a tasty and healthy meal, serve the stuffed bell peppers with quinoa and feta.

Nutrition (per serving, one stuffed pepper):

- Calories: ~300
- Protein: ~10g
- Carbohydrates: ~35g
- Fiber: ~8g
- Fat: ~15g

PEACH AND CHIA SEED PARFAIT

Ingredients:

- 1 cup Greek yoghurt (plain or vanilla)
- 1 ripe peach, sliced
- 2 tablespoons chia seeds
- 2 tablespoons honey or maple syrup
- Granola for topping (optional)

Instructions:

1. Layer Greek yoghurt, sliced peaches, chia seeds, and honey or maple syrup in a glass or jar.
2. As many times as you want.

3. You can add some granola on top of the parfait if you want.
4. The peach and chia seed dessert is a tasty and refreshing way to start the day or end a meal.

Nutrition (per serving):

- Calories: ~250
- Protein: ~10g
- Carbohydrates: ~30g
- Fiber: ~5g
- Fat: ~10g

CAULIFLOWER AND CHICKPEA TACOS

Ingredients:

- 2 cups cauliflower florets
- 1 can (15 oz) chickpeas, drained and rinsed
- 1 teaspoon chilli powder
- 1/2 teaspoon ground cumin
- 1/4 teaspoon smoked paprika
- Salt and pepper to taste
- 8 small corn or whole wheat tortillas
- Toppings: diced avocado, chopped fresh cilantro, lime wedges

Instructions:

1. Turn the oven on and set it to 400°F (200°C).

2. Mix the cauliflower pieces and chickpeas with olive oil, chilli powder, ground cumin, smoked paprika, salt, and pepper.
3. Spread the cauliflower and chickpeas on a baking sheet and roast for about 20 to 25 minutes until the cauliflower is soft and slightly crispy.
4. Follow the directions on the package to heat the tortillas.
5. Spread roasted cauliflower and chickpea filling on each tortilla to make a taco.
6. Add toppings like diced avocado and chopped fresh parsley if you want.
7. The cauliflower and chickpea tacos should be served with pieces of lime.

Nutrition (per serving, two tacos):

- Calories: ~300
- Protein: ~10g
- Carbohydrates: ~45g
- Fiber: ~12g
- Fat: ~6g

HIGH-FIBER BANANA NUT WAFFLES

Ingredients:

- 1 1/2 cups whole wheat flour
- 1/2 cup rolled oats
- 1/4 cup ground flaxseed
- 2 teaspoons baking powder
- 1/2 teaspoon ground cinnamon
- 1/4 teaspoon salt

- 2 ripe bananas, mashed
- 1 3/4 cups almond milk (or any milk of choice)
- 1/4 cup chopped walnuts
- 2 tablespoons honey or maple syrup
- 1 teaspoon vanilla extract

Instructions:

1. Follow the directions on the box to heat a waffle iron.
2. Whisk the whole wheat flour, rolled oats, flaxseed, baking powder, cinnamon, and salt in a big bowl.
3. Mix the mashed bananas, almond milk, chopped walnuts, honey or maple syrup, and vanilla extract in a separate bowl.
4. Pour the wet ingredients into the dry ingredients and stir until just mixed.
5. Use a little oil or nonstick cooking spray to grease the waffle pan.
6. Pour the waffle batter onto the waffle iron, which has already been heated, and cook according to the guidelines on the box.
7. Banana-nut waffles that are high in fibre can be topped with your favourite things.

Nutrition (per waffle, recipe makes about six waffles):

- Calories: ~250
- Protein: ~8g
- Carbohydrates: ~40g
- Fiber: ~8g
- Fat: ~8g

BLACK BEAN AND CORN TAMALES

Ingredients:

- 1 cup masa harina (corn masa flour)
- 1/2 teaspoon salt
- 1/2 teaspoon baking powder
- 1/2 cup vegetable broth
- 1/4 cup olive oil or melted coconut oil
- 1 can (15 oz) black beans, drained and rinsed
- 1 cup corn kernels (fresh, frozen, or canned)
- 1 teaspoon chilli powder
- 1/2 teaspoon ground cumin
- Salt and pepper to taste
- Corn husks soaked in warm water

Instructions:

1. Whisk the masa harina, salt, and baking powder in a large bowl.
2. Gradually add the veggie broth and olive oil, mixing until the dough comes together.
3. Mix the black beans, corn kernels, chilli powder, ground cumin, salt, and pepper in a separate bowl.
4. Put a thin layer of masa dough in the middle of a wet corn husk, leaving space around the sides.
5. On top of the masa dough, put a spoonful of the black bean and corn filling.
6. Fold the sides of the corn husk over the filling, then fold the bottom up to close the tamale.
7. Do the same thing with the rest of the dough, filling, and corn husks.
8. Put the tamales in a steamer basket so they stand up straight.

9. Steam the tamales over hot water for about 45 to 60 minutes, or until the masa dough is cooked and firm.
10. Let the tamales cool a bit before you open them and serve them.

Nutrition (per tamale, recipe makes about six tamales):
- Calories: ~300
- Protein: ~8g
- Carbohydrates: ~45g
- Fiber: ~8g
- Fat: ~10g

FIBER-PACKED TROPICAL FRUIT SMOOTHIE

Ingredients:
- 1 cup mixed tropical fruits (mango, pineapple, papaya)
- 1 banana
- 1/2 cup Greek yoghurt (plain or vanilla)
- 1 tablespoon chia seeds
- 1 cup almond milk (or any milk of choice)
- Honey or maple syrup to taste (optional)

Instructions:
1. Mix tropical fruits, a banana, Greek yoghurt, chia seeds, and almond milk in a blender.
2. Mix until creamy and smooth.
3. If you want, you can add honey or maple syrup to sweeten it.
4. Pour the tropical fruit smoothie, which is full of fibre, into cups and enjoy.

Nutrition (per serving):

- Calories: ~250
- Protein: ~8g
- Carbohydrates: ~45g
- Fiber: ~10g
- Fat: ~5g

LENTIL AND VEGETABLE STIR-FRY WITH PEANUT SAUCE

Ingredients:

- 1 cup green or brown lentils, uncooked
- 2 cups mixed vegetables (bell peppers, broccoli, carrots, snap peas, etc.)
- 1 tablespoon olive oil
- 2 cloves garlic, minced
- 1 teaspoon grated ginger
- 1/4 cup peanut butter
- 2 tablespoons soy sauce
- 1 tablespoon honey or maple syrup
- Juice of 1 lime
- Crushed red pepper flakes (optional)
- Chopped peanuts for garnish (optional)

Instructions:

1. Rinse the lentils with cold water and put them to the side.
2. Follow the directions on the package to cook the lentils in a pot. Drain and put away.
3. Olive oil is heated over medium heat in a large pot.

4. Chop some garlic and grate some ginger. For about a minute, sauté until the food smells good.
5. Add the mixed veggies and cook for 5–7 minutes until they soften.
6. Mix peanut butter, soy sauce, honey or maple syrup, lime juice, and red pepper flakes, if using, in a bowl with a spoon.
7. Pour the peanut sauce over the veggies and stir well.
8. Cooked lentils should be added to the pan and stirred together.
9. Cook for another 2–3 minutes to make sure everything is hot.
10. The lentil and veggie stir-fry can be served with peanut sauce and chopped peanuts.

Nutrition (per serving):
- Calories: ~350
- Protein: ~15g
- Carbohydrates: ~40g
- Fiber: ~12g
- Fat: ~15g

QUINOA AND SPINACH STUFFED PORTOBELLO MUSHROOMS

Ingredients:
- 4 large portobello mushrooms, stems removed
- 1 cup cooked quinoa
- 1 cup chopped fresh spinach
- 1/2 cup diced tomatoes

- 1/4 cup diced red onion
- 1/4 cup crumbled feta cheese
- 2 tablespoons balsamic vinegar
- 2 tablespoons olive oil
- Salt and pepper to taste

Instructions:

1. Turn the oven on and set it to 375°F (190°C).
2. Place the portobello mushrooms, gill side up, on a baking sheet.
3. Mix the cooked rice, chopped fresh spinach, diced tomatoes, diced red onion, and crumbled feta cheese in a bowl.
4. Pour olive oil and balsamic vinegar over the rice mixture. Add salt and pepper to taste.
5. Put the rice mixture into the portobello mushrooms and pack it in with your fingers.
6. Bake in an oven that has already been warm for 20 to 25 minutes or until the mushrooms are soft and the filling is hot.
7. Serve the portobello mushrooms stuffed with rice and spinach as a filling dish.

Nutrition (per serving, one stuffed mushroom):

- Calories: ~250
- Protein: ~10g
- Carbohydrates: ~30g
- Fiber: ~8g
- Fat: ~10g

MIXED BERRY CHIA SEED YOGURT BOWL

Ingredients:

- 1 cup Greek yoghurt (plain or vanilla)
- 1/2 cup mixed berries (blueberries, raspberries, strawberries)
- 2 tablespoons chia seeds
- 1 tablespoon honey or maple syrup
- Chopped nuts for topping (optional)

Instructions:

1. Put Greek yoghurt, mixed berries, and chia seeds in a bowl and stack them up.
2. Honey or maple syrup can be drizzled on the yoghurt and berries.
3. If you want, you can put chopped nuts on top of the yoghurt.
4. You can eat the mixed berry chia seed yoghurt bowl for breakfast or as a healthy snack.

Nutrition (per serving):

- Calories: ~250
- Protein: ~15g
- Carbohydrates: ~30g
- Fiber: ~8g
- Fat: ~10g

ROASTED VEGETABLE AND HUMMUS WRAP

Ingredients:

- 2 large whole wheat tortillas
- 1 cup roasted vegetables (bell peppers, zucchini, eggplant, etc.)
- 1/2 cup hummus
- 1/4 cup crumbled feta cheese
- Fresh spinach leaves
- Olive oil for brushing

Instructions:

1. Follow the directions on the package to heat the whole wheat tortillas.
2. On each tortilla, spread 1/4 cup of hummus.
3. On top of the hummus, lay down raw spinach leaves.
4. On each tortilla, put some roasted veggies.
5. Crumble some feta cheese on top.
6. Pour some olive oil over the veggies.
7. To make wraps, tightly roll the tortillas.

Nutrition (per wrap):

- Calories: ~300
- Protein: ~10g
- Carbohydrates: ~40g
- Fiber: ~10g
- Fat: ~12g

FIBER-RICH CHOCOLATE PROTEIN PANCAKES

Ingredients:

- 1 cup whole wheat flour
- 1/4 cup cocoa powder
- 1/4 cup ground flaxseed
- 1 scoop of chocolate protein powder
- 1 teaspoon baking powder
- 1/2 teaspoon baking soda
- 1/2 teaspoon ground cinnamon
- 1 cup buttermilk or milk of choice
- 1/4 cup Greek yogurt
- 1/4 cup unsweetened applesauce
- 1 egg
- 1 teaspoon vanilla extract
- Dark chocolate chips for topping (optional)

Instructions:

1. Mix the whole wheat flour, cocoa powder, ground flaxseed, chocolate protein powder, baking powder, baking soda, and ground cinnamon in a big bowl with a whisk.
2. Mix the buttermilk, Greek yoghurt, unsweetened applesauce, egg, and vanilla extract in another bowl.
3. Pour the wet ingredients into the dry ingredients and stir until just mixed.
4. Heat a pan or grill that doesn't stick to medium heat.
5. For each pancake, pour 1/4 cup of batter into the pan.
6. Cook until bubbles appear on the top, then flip and cook for 1-2 minutes.

7. If you want, you can put dark chocolate chips on top of the pancakes.

Nutrition (per serving, the recipe makes about eight pancakes):

- Calories: ~300
- Protein: ~15g
- Carbohydrates: ~40g
- Fiber: ~8g
- Fat: ~10g

MOROCCAN CHICKPEA AND VEGETABLE TAGINE

Ingredients:

- 1 cup dried chickpeas, soaked and cooked (or one can of chickpeas, drained and rinsed)
- 2 cups diced vegetables (carrots, bell peppers, zucchini, etc.)
- 1 onion, chopped
- 2 cloves garlic, minced
- 1 teaspoon ground cumin
- 1 teaspoon ground coriander
- 1/2 teaspoon ground cinnamon
- 1/4 teaspoon ground turmeric
- 1/4 teaspoon cayenne pepper (adjust to taste)
- 1 can (14 oz) diced tomatoes
- 1 cup vegetable broth
- 1/4 cup dried apricots, chopped

- 1/4 cup sliced almonds
- Fresh cilantro for garnish
- Cooked couscous or quinoa for serving

Instructions:

1. Heat olive oil in a large pan or tagine pot and cook the chopped onion until it turns transparent.
2. Mix in chopped garlic, ground cumin, coriander, cinnamon, turmeric, and cayenne pepper. Cook for about a minute or two until the smell is pleasant.
3. Add the diced veggies and cook for 5 to 7 minutes or until they soften.
4. Mix in the diced tomatoes, veggie broth, and already cooked chickpeas.
5. Bring the mixture to a boil and cook for 15 to 20 minutes to let the flavours blend.
6. Add the sliced almonds and chopped dried apricots.
7. Serve the chickpea and veggie tagine from Morocco with cooked couscous or quinoa and fresh cilantro on top.

Nutrition (per serving):

- Calories: ~350
- Protein: ~15g
- Carbohydrates: ~55g
- Fiber: ~15g
- Fat: ~8g

TOMATO BASIL LENTIL SOUP

Ingredients:

- 1 cup green or brown lentils, uncooked
- 1 onion, chopped
- 2 cloves garlic, minced
- 1 can (28 oz) crushed tomatoes
- 4 cups vegetable broth
- 1 teaspoon dried basil
- 1/2 teaspoon dried oregano
- 1/4 teaspoon red pepper flakes (adjust to taste)
- Salt and pepper to taste
- Fresh basil leaves for garnish

Instructions:

1. Rinse the lentils with cold water and put them to the side.
2. Cook the chopped onion in olive oil until it becomes clear.
3. Add chopped garlic and cook for about a minute or until the garlic smells good.
4. Mix the crushed tomatoes, veggie broth, dried basil, oregano, red pepper flakes, salt, and pepper.
5. Bring the soup to a boil, boil it, and let it cook for 20 to 25 minutes.
6. Add the lentils that have been cleaned to the soup and keep it simmering for another 20–25 minutes or until the lentils are soft.
7. Taste it and, if necessary, change the flavour.
8. Fresh basil leaves can be used to decorate the tomato basil lentil soup.

Nutrition (per serving):

- Calories: ~250
- Protein: ~15g
- Carbohydrates: ~45g
- Fiber: ~15g
- Fat: ~2g

HIGH FIBER ALMOND BUTTER MUFFINS

Ingredients:

- 1 1/2 cups whole wheat flour
- 1/4 cup ground flaxseed
- 1 teaspoon baking powder
- 1/2 teaspoon baking soda
- 1/2 teaspoon ground cinnamon
- 1/4 teaspoon salt
- 1/2 cup almond butter
- 1/4 cup honey or maple syrup
- 1 cup almond milk (or any milk of choice)
- 1 egg
- 1 teaspoon vanilla extract
- 1/2 cup chopped dates or raisins
- Chopped almonds for topping (optional)

Instructions:

1. Turn the oven on and set it to 350°F (175°C). Use paper cups to line a muffin pan.
2. Whisk the whole wheat flour, ground flaxseed, baking powder, baking soda, ground cinnamon, and salt in a large bowl.
3. Mix the honey or maple syrup, egg, almond milk, vanilla extract, and almond butter in another bowl.
4. Pour the wet ingredients into the dry ingredients and stir until just mixed.
5. Mix in the chopped dates or raisins with care.

6. Put the same amount of batter in each muffin cup.
7. If you want, you can sprinkle each muffin with chopped nuts.
8. Bake for about 18 to 20 minutes or until a toothpick stuck in the middle comes out clean.
9. Let the muffins cool down before you serve them.

Nutrition (per muffin, recipe makes about 12 muffins):

- Calories: ~250
- Protein: ~8g
- Carbohydrates: ~35g
- Fiber: ~8g
- Fat: ~10g

STUFFED ZUCCHINI WITH QUINOA AND TOMATO SAUCE

Ingredients:

- 4 large zucchini
- 1 cup cooked quinoa
- 1/2 cup diced tomatoes
- 1/4 cup diced red onion
- 1/4 cup chopped fresh parsley
- 2 cloves garlic, minced
- 1/4 cup grated Parmesan cheese
- Salt and pepper to taste
- Olive oil for brushing
- Tomato sauce for serving

Instructions:

1. Turn the oven on and set it to 375°F (190°C).
2. Cut the zucchini in half along its length and scoop out the inside to make zucchini boats.
3. Mix the cooked quinoa, tomatoes, red onion, chopped fresh parsley, crushed garlic, grated Parmesan cheese, salt, and pepper in a bowl.
4. Put the zucchini boats in a baking dish and brush them with olive oil.
5. Put some of the rice mixture into each zucchini boat.
6. Bake in an oven that has already been warm for 20 to 25 minutes or until the zucchini is soft and the filling is hot.
7. Serve the zucchinis that have been stuffed with rice and tomato sauce.

Nutrition (per serving, two stuffed zucchini halves):
- Calories: ~300
- Protein: ~15g
- Carbohydrates: ~40g
- Fiber: ~10g
- Fat: ~10g

GRILLED VEGGIE AND HUMMUS PANINI

Ingredients:
- 4 slices whole wheat bread
- 1/2 cup hummus
- 1 cup grilled vegetables (zucchini, bell peppers, eggplant, etc.)
- 1/4 cup crumbled feta cheese

- Olive oil or cooking spray

Instructions:

1. Heat a grill pan or sandwich press.
2. On one side of each piece of bread, spread hummus.
3. Stack two slices of bread with grilled veggies and crumbled feta cheese.
4. Add the other slices of bread on top to make sandwiches.
5. Brush a little olive oil or cooking spray on the outside of the sandwiches.
6. Use the panini press or grill pan to cook the sandwiches until the bread is warmed and the filling is hot.
7. The sandwich should be cut in half and served.

Nutrition (per panini):

- Calories: ~300
- Protein: ~10g
- Carbohydrates: ~40g
- Fiber: ~8g
- Fat: ~12g

FIBER-PACKED MIXED BERRY BREAKFAST BARS

Ingredients:

- 1 1/2 cups rolled oats
- 1/2 cup whole wheat flour
- 1/4 cup ground flaxseed
- 1/2 teaspoon baking soda
- 1/2 teaspoon ground cinnamon

- 1/4 teaspoon salt
- 1/2 cup almond butter or peanut butter
- 1/4 cup honey or maple syrup
- 1/4 cup unsweetened applesauce
- 1 egg
- 1 teaspoon vanilla extract
- 1 cup mixed berries (blueberries, raspberries, strawberries)
- Chopped nuts for topping (optional)

Instructions:

1. Turn the oven on and set it to 350°F (175°C). Line a baking dish with parchment paper, leaving a little extra so it will be easy to remove.
2. Mix the rolled oats, whole wheat flour, ground flaxseed, baking soda, cinnamon powder, and salt in a big bowl.
3. Mix almond butter, honey or maple syrup, applesauce that hasn't been flavoured, an egg, and vanilla extract in another bowl.
4. Pour the liquids into the dry ingredients and stir until everything is well-mixed.
5. Gently mix in the berries.
6. Spread the mixture thoroughly in the ready baking dish.
7. If you want, sprinkle chopped nuts on top.
8. Bake the bars for about 20 to 25 minutes or until golden brown and hard.
9. Please wait until the bars have cooled down to cut them into squares.

Nutrition (per bar, recipe makes about 12 bars):

- Calories: ~200
- Protein: ~6g
- Carbohydrates: ~25g

- Fiber: ~6g
- Fat: ~9g

SPAGHETTI SQUASH WITH CHICKPEA ALFREDO

Ingredients:

- 1 medium spaghetti squash
- 1 can (15 oz) chickpeas, drained and rinsed
- 1 cup unsweetened almond milk (or any milk of choice)
- 1/4 cup nutritional yeast
- 2 cloves garlic, minced
- 1 tablespoon olive oil
- 1/2 teaspoon ground nutmeg
- Salt and pepper to taste
- Chopped parsley for garnish

Instructions:

1. Turn the oven on and set it to 400°F (200°C).
2. Split the spaghetti squash in half lengthwise and scoop out the seeds.
3. Place the squash halves, cut side down, on a baking sheet. Roast in the oven for 40 to 45 minutes until the meat is soft and easily scraped into "spaghetti" strands with a fork.
4. Make the chickpea Alfredo sauce while the squash is cooking.
5. Mix chickpeas, almond milk, nutritional yeast, minced garlic, olive oil, ground nutmeg, salt, and pepper in a mixer. Mix until creamy and smooth.

6. Place the sauce in a pot and heat it on low.
7. When the spaghetti squash is done cooking, use a fork to scrape the meat into "spaghetti"-like strands.
8. Pour the chickpea Alfredo sauce over the spaghetti squash and stir to coat.
9. Serve the spaghetti squash with chopped parsley on top of the chickpea Alfredo.

Nutrition (per serving):
- Calories: ~300
- Protein: ~12g
- Carbohydrates: ~40g
- Fiber: ~10g
- Fat: ~10g

THREE-BEAN AND QUINOA BOWL

Ingredients:
- 1/2 cup cooked quinoa
- 1/2 cup black beans, cooked or canned (drained and rinsed)
- 1/2 cup kidney beans, cooked or canned (drained and rinsed)
- 1/2 cup chickpeas, cooked or canned (drained and rinsed)
- 1 cup mixed vegetables (bell peppers, corn, red onion, etc.)
- 2 tablespoons chopped fresh cilantro
- 2 tablespoons lime juice
- 1 tablespoon olive oil

- 1/2 teaspoon ground cumin
- Salt and pepper to taste
- Avocado slices for topping (optional)

Instructions:

1. Cooked quinoa, black beans, kidney beans, chickpeas, mixed veggies, and chopped fresh cilantro are mixed in a bowl.
2. Mix lime juice, olive oil, cumin powder, salt, and pepper in a different bowl with a whisk.
3. Pour the dressing over the rice and beans, then toss everything together.
4. If you want, you can put avocado pieces on top.

Nutrition (per serving):

- Calories: ~300
- Protein: ~15g
- Carbohydrates: ~45g
- Fiber: ~12g
- Fat: ~8g

ROASTED RED PEPPER AND AVOCADO SANDWICH

Ingredients:

- 4 slices whole grain bread
- 1 large ripe avocado, sliced
- 1/2 cup roasted red pepper strips
- Handful of baby spinach leaves
- 1 tablespoon balsamic vinegar

- Salt and pepper to taste

Instructions:

1. The pieces of whole-grain bread should be toasted.
2. Stack slices of avocado on two pieces of bread.
3. Red pepper pieces and baby spinach leaves go on top.
4. Balsamic vinegar should be drizzled over the toppings.
5. Add salt and pepper to taste.
6. Add the other slices of bread on top to make sandwiches.

Nutrition (per sandwich):

- Calories: ~300
- Protein: ~8g
- Carbohydrates: ~35g
- Fiber: ~10g
- Fat: ~15g

FIBER-RICH BLUEBERRY CHIA SEED SMOOTHIE

Ingredients:

- 1 cup frozen blueberries
- 1 banana
- 1 tablespoon chia seeds
- 1 cup almond milk (or any milk of choice)
- 1/4 cup Greek yoghurt (plain or vanilla)
- 1 tablespoon honey or maple syrup
- Handful of spinach leaves (optional)

Instructions:

1. Mix frozen blueberries, bananas, chia seeds, almond milk, Greek yoghurt, honey or maple syrup, and spinach leaves, if you're using them, in a mixer.
2. Mix until creamy and smooth.
3. Pour the blueberry chia seed drink, which is high in fibre, into glasses and enjoy.

Nutrition (per serving):

- Calories: ~250
- Protein: ~8g
- Carbohydrates: ~40g
- Fiber: ~10g
- Fat: ~8g

COCONUT LENTIL AND VEGETABLE CURRY

Ingredients:

- 1 cup dried green or brown lentils, soaked and cooked (or one can of lentils, drained and rinsed)
- 1 onion, chopped
- 2 cloves garlic, minced
- 1 tablespoon grated ginger
- 1 tablespoon curry powder
- 1/2 teaspoon ground turmeric
- 1/2 teaspoon ground cumin
- 1/4 teaspoon cayenne pepper (adjust to taste)
- 1 can (14 oz) coconut milk

- 2 cups mixed vegetables (carrots, bell peppers, peas, etc.)
- 1 tablespoon olive oil
- Fresh cilantro for garnish
- Cooked brown rice or quinoa for serving

Instructions:

1. Cook the chopped onion in olive oil in a large pot until it turns transparent.
2. Chop some garlic and grate some ginger. Cook for about a minute or until the smell is pleasant.
3. Add the curry powder, turmeric powder, cumin powder, and cayenne pepper.
4. Add the lentils that have been cooked, the coconut milk, and the veggies.
5. Allow the curry to simmer for 15 to 20 minutes to let the flavours mix and the veggies soften.
6. Coconut lentil and veggie curry can be served with cooked brown rice, quinoa, and fresh cilantro.

Nutrition (per serving):

- Calories: ~350
- Protein: ~15g
- Carbohydrates: ~40g
- Fiber: ~12g
- Fat: ~15g

QUINOA AND BLACK BEAN STUFFED MUSHROOMS

Ingredients:

- 12 large button or cremini mushrooms, stems removed
- 1 cup cooked quinoa
- 1/2 cup black beans, cooked or canned (drained and rinsed)
- 1/4 cup diced red onion
- 1/4 cup diced tomatoes
- 1/4 cup chopped fresh cilantro
- 1/4 cup shredded cheddar cheese
- 1 tablespoon olive oil
- 1/2 teaspoon ground cumin
- Salt and pepper to taste

Instructions:

1. Turn the oven on and set it to 375°F (190°C).
2. The mushroom caps should be put on a baking sheet.
3. Mix the cooked quinoa, black beans, diced red onion, diced tomatoes, chopped fresh cilantro, shredded cheddar cheese, olive oil, ground cumin, salt, and pepper in a bowl.
4. Fill each mushroom cap with the quinoa filling.
5. Bake in an oven heated for about 15 to 20 minutes or until the mushrooms are soft and the sauce is hot.
6. The mushrooms filled with quinoa and black beans are a tasty starter or main dish.

Nutrition (per serving, three stuffed mushrooms):

- Calories: ~250
- Protein: ~12g
- Carbohydrates: ~30g
- Fiber: ~8g
- Fat: ~10g

BLACK BEAN AND CORN SALAD WITH LIME VINAIGRETTE

Ingredients:

- 1 can (15 oz) black beans, drained and rinsed
- 1 cup corn kernels (fresh, frozen, or canned)
- 1/2 cup diced red onion
- 1/2 cup diced bell peppers (any colour)
- 1/4 cup chopped fresh cilantro
- Juice of 2 limes
- 2 tablespoons olive oil
- 1 teaspoon ground cumin
- Salt and pepper to taste

Instructions:

1. Mix black beans, corn kernels, diced red onion, bell peppers, and chopped fresh cilantro in a big bowl.
2. Mix lime juice, olive oil, ground cumin, salt, and pepper in a small bowl with a whisk.
3. Pour the lime dressing over the beans and corn and toss to coat.
4. Use the black bean and corn salad as a side dish or a filling for salads or tacos.

Nutrition (per serving):

- Calories: ~200
- Protein: ~8g
- Carbohydrates: ~30g
- Fiber: ~10g
- Fat: ~8g

HIGH-FIBER PEANUT BUTTER BANANA PANCAKES

Ingredients:

- 1 cup whole wheat flour
- 1/4 cup ground flaxseed
- 1 teaspoon baking powder
- 1/2 teaspoon baking soda
- 1/2 teaspoon ground cinnamon
- 1/4 teaspoon salt
- 1 cup buttermilk or milk of choice
- 1/4 cup natural peanut butter
- 1 ripe banana, mashed
- 1 egg
- 1 teaspoon vanilla extract
- Sliced bananas and chopped peanuts for topping (optional)

Instructions:

1. Whisk the whole wheat flour, ground flaxseed, baking powder, baking soda, ground cinnamon, and salt in a large bowl.
2. Mix buttermilk, peanut butter, banana puree, egg, vanilla extract, and vanilla extract in another bowl.
3. Pour the wet ingredients into the dry ingredients and stir until just mixed.
4. Heat a pan or grill that doesn't stick to medium heat.
5. For each pancake, pour 1/4 cup of batter into the pan.
6. Cook until bubbles appear on the top, then flip and cook for 1-2 minutes.

7. If you want, you can put sliced bananas and chopped peanuts on top of the pancakes.

Nutrition (per serving, recipe makes about 8 pancakes):

- Calories: ~300
- Protein: ~10g
- Carbohydrates: ~40g
- Fiber: ~8g
- Fat: ~10g

RATATOUILLE STUFFED BELL PEPPERS

Ingredients:

- 4 large bell peppers, any colour
- 1 cup diced eggplant
- 1 cup diced zucchini
- 1 cup diced red onion
- 1 cup diced bell peppers (any colour)
- 1 cup diced tomatoes
- 2 cloves garlic, minced
- 2 tablespoons olive oil
- 1 teaspoon dried thyme
- 1 teaspoon dried oregano
- Salt and pepper to taste
- Grated Parmesan cheese for topping (optional)

Instructions:

1. Turn the oven on and set it to 375°F (190°C).

2. Remove the seeds and skins from the bell peppers and cut off the tops.
3. Olive oil is heated over medium heat in a large pot.
4. Put chopped eggplant, zucchini, red onion, and bell peppers in the pan. Sauté the veggies for about 5 to 7 minutes or until they get soft.
5. Mix in diced tomatoes, chopped garlic, dried thyme, dried oregano, salt, and pepper. Keep cooking for another 2 minutes.
6. Fill the bell peppers with the ratatouille filling.
7. Put the bell peppers stuffed in a baking dish and cover them with aluminium foil.
8. Bake for about 25 to 30 minutes in an oven that has already been warm or until the peppers are soft.
9. Take off the foil and, if you want, put grated Parmesan cheese on top. Bake for another 5 minutes or until the cheese is bubbly and melted.

Nutrition (per serving, one stuffed bell pepper):

- Calories: ~250
- Protein: ~6g
- Carbohydrates: ~30g
- Fiber: ~10g
- Fat: ~12g

MIXED BERRY CHIA SEED PUDDING

Ingredients:

- 1/4 cup chia seeds
- 1 cup almond milk (or any milk of choice)
- 1/2 teaspoon vanilla extract

- 1 tablespoon honey or maple syrup
- 1/2 cup mixed berries (blueberries, raspberries, strawberries)

Instructions:

1. Whisk chia seeds, almond milk, vanilla extract, and honey or maple syrup together in a bowl.
2. Let the mixture sit for about 10 minutes, and then whisk it again to break up any clumps.
3. Cover the bowl and put it in the fridge for at least 4 hours or overnight.
4. Give the chia seed pudding a good stir before you serve it.
5. Before serving, sprinkle mixed berries on top.

Nutrition (per serving):

- Calories: ~200
- Protein: ~6g
- Carbohydrates: ~25g
- Fiber: ~12g
- Fat: ~8g

ROASTED VEGETABLE AND HUMMUS PANINI

Ingredients:

- 4 slices whole wheat bread
- 1/2 cup hummus
- 1 cup roasted vegetables (zucchini, bell peppers, eggplant, etc.)
- 1/4 cup crumbled feta cheese

- Olive oil or cooking spray

Instructions:

1. Heat a grill pan or sandwich press.
2. On one side of each piece of bread, spread hummus.
3. On two slices of bread, stack roasted veggies and crumbled feta cheese.
4. Add the other slices of bread on top to make sandwiches.
5. Brush a little olive oil or cooking spray on the outside of the sandwiches.
6. Use the panini press or grill pan to cook the sandwiches until the bread is warmed and the filling is hot.
7. The sandwich should be cut in half and served.

Nutrition (per panini):

- Calories: ~300
- Protein: ~10g
- Carbohydrates: ~40g
- Fiber: ~8g
- Fat: ~12g

FIBER-PACKED CHOCOLATE BANANA OAT BARS

Ingredients:

- 2 ripe bananas, mashed
- 1/4 cup honey or maple syrup
- 1/4 cup natural peanut butter
- 1 teaspoon vanilla extract
- 1 1/2 cups rolled oats

- 1/4 cup ground flaxseed
- 1/4 cup cocoa powder
- 1/2 teaspoon baking powder
- 1/4 teaspoon salt
- 1/4 cup dark chocolate chips

Instructions:

1. Turn the oven on and set it to 350°F (175°C). Line a baking dish with parchment paper, leaving a little extra so it will be easy to remove.
2. Mix mashed bananas, honey or maple syrup, peanut butter, and vanilla extract until well.
3. Mix rolled oats, ground flaxseed, cocoa powder, baking powder, and salt in another bowl.
4. Mix the wet and dry ingredients until everything is well combined.
5. Add the dark chocolate chips to the mixture.
6. Spread the mixture thoroughly in the ready baking dish.
7. Bake the bars for 20 to 25 minutes or until they feel stiff when you touch them.
8. Please wait until the bars have cooled down to cut them into squares.

Nutrition (per bar, recipe makes about 12 bars):

- Calories: ~200
- Protein: ~6g
- Carbohydrates: ~30g
- Fiber: ~8g
- Fat: ~8g

LENTIL AND VEGETABLE STIR-FRY WITH TERIYAKI SAUCE

Ingredients:

- 1 cup cooked green or brown lentils
- 2 cups mixed vegetables (broccoli, bell peppers, carrots, snap peas, etc.)
- 1/4 cup teriyaki sauce
- 2 tablespoons low-sodium soy sauce
- 1 tablespoon olive oil
- 2 cloves garlic, minced
- 1 teaspoon grated ginger
- Sliced green onions for garnish
- Cooked brown rice for serving

Instructions:

1. Olive oil should be heated in a big skillet or wok over medium-high heat.
2. Chop some garlic and grate some ginger. Cook for about a minute or until the smell is pleasant.
3. Stir-fry the mixed veggies for about 3–5 minutes or until they become soft.
4. Stir in the cooked lentils, low-sodium soy sauce, and teriyaki sauce. Cook for another 2–3 minutes until everything is hot.
5. Serve the stir-fried lentils and vegetables over cooked brown rice and top with thinly sliced green onions.

Nutrition (per serving):

- Calories: ~300
- Protein: ~10g
- Carbohydrates: ~45g

- Fiber: ~10g
- Fat: ~8g

SPAGHETTI SQUASH WITH LENTIL PESTO

Ingredients:

- 1 medium spaghetti squash
- 1 cup cooked green or brown lentils
- 1 cup fresh basil leaves
- 1/4 cup grated Parmesan cheese
- 1/4 cup pine nuts
- 2 cloves garlic
- Juice of 1 lemon
- 1/4 cup olive oil
- Salt and pepper to taste

Instructions:

1. Turn the oven on and set it to 400°F (200°C).
2. Split the spaghetti squash in half lengthwise and scoop out the seeds.
3. Place the squash halves, cut side down, on a baking sheet. Roast in the oven for 40 to 45 minutes until the meat is soft and easily scraped into "spaghetti" strands with a fork.
4. Make the bean pesto while the squash is in the oven.
5. Mix basil leaves, chopped Parmesan cheese, pine nuts, garlic, lemon juice, olive oil, salt, and pepper in a food processor. Mix until it's smooth.
6. Mix the cooked lentils and lentil pesto in a bowl.

7. When the spaghetti squash is done cooking, use a fork to scrape the meat into "spaghetti"-like strands.
8. Mix the lentil pesto mixture with the spaghetti squash.
9. Lentil sauce goes well with spaghetti squash.

Nutrition (per serving):

- Calories: ~300
- Protein: ~12g
- Carbohydrates: ~40g
- Fiber: ~10g
- Fat: ~12g

THREE-BEAN AND BROWN RICE SALAD

Ingredients:

- 1 cup cooked brown rice
- 1/2 cup cooked black beans
- 1/2 cup cooked kidney beans
- 1/2 cup cooked chickpeas
- 1/2 cup diced bell peppers (any colour)
- 1/4 cup diced red onion
- 1/4 cup chopped fresh parsley
- 2 tablespoons olive oil
- Juice of 1 lemon
- 1 teaspoon ground cumin
- Salt and pepper to taste

Instructions:

1. Cooked brown rice, black beans, kidney beans, chickpeas, diced bell peppers, diced red onion, and chopped fresh parsley are all mixed together in a big bowl.
2. Whisk the olive oil, lemon juice, cumin powder, salt, and pepper in a small bowl.
3. Pour the sauce over the beans and rice mixture and stir to coat.
4. The three-bean and brown rice salad can be a side meal or a main course. It is both filling and healthy.

Nutrition (per serving):

- Calories: ~300
- Protein: ~10g
- Carbohydrates: ~45g
- Fiber: ~10g
- Fat: ~8g

ROASTED RED PEPPER AND AVOCADO WRAP

Ingredients:

- 1 large whole wheat tortilla
- 1/2 cup roasted red pepper strips
- 1/2 avocado, sliced
- Handful of baby spinach leaves
- 2 tablespoons hummus
- Salt and pepper to taste

Instructions:

1. Put the whole wheat tortilla on a clean surface and spread it flat.
2. The hummus was spread on the bread.
3. Put pieces of roasted red pepper, slices of avocado, baby spinach leaves, salt, and pepper in a dish in layers.
4. Fold the tortilla's sides in, then roll it up tightly from the bottom.
5. The wrap should be cut in half and served.

Nutrition (per wrap):

- Calories: ~300
- Protein: ~8g
- Carbohydrates: ~40g
- Fiber: ~10g
- Fat: ~12g

FIBER-RICH GREEN SMOOTHIE BOWL

Ingredients:

- 1 frozen banana
- 1 cup spinach leaves
- 1/2 cup frozen mixed berries (blueberries, raspberries, strawberries)
- 1/2 avocado
- 1 cup almond milk (or any milk of choice)
- 1 tablespoon chia seeds
- Toppings: sliced banana, chia seeds, granola, nuts

Instructions:

1. Mix a frozen banana, spinach leaves, frozen mixed berries, an avocado, almond milk, and chia seeds in a blender.
2. Mix until creamy and smooth.
3. The green juice should be poured into a bowl.
4. Banana slices, chia seeds, granola, and nuts go on top.

Nutrition (per serving):

- Calories: ~350
- Protein: ~8g
- Carbohydrates: ~45g
- Fiber: ~12g
- Fat: ~15g

CHICKPEA AND VEGETABLE COCONUT CURRY

Ingredients:

- 1 can (15 oz) chickpeas, drained and rinsed
- 2 cups mixed vegetables (bell peppers, carrots, peas, etc.)
- 1 can (14 oz) coconut milk
- 1 tablespoon curry powder
- 1 teaspoon ground turmeric
- 1/2 teaspoon ground cumin
- 1/4 teaspoon cayenne pepper (adjust to taste)
- 1 tablespoon olive oil
- 1 onion, chopped
- 2 cloves garlic, minced
- Salt and pepper to taste

- Fresh cilantro for garnish
- Cooked brown rice for serving

Instructions:

1. Olive oil is heated over medium heat in a large pot.
2. Cook the onion until it becomes clear.
3. Mix in the chopped garlic, curry powder, turmeric powder, cumin powder, and cayenne pepper. Cook for about a minute or until the smell is pleasant.
4. Put a variety of veggies and chickpeas in the pan. Sauté the veggies for about 5 to 7 minutes or until they get soft.
5. Stir in the coconut milk and let the curry cook for 10 to 15 minutes.
6. Add salt and pepper to taste.
7. Chickpea and veggie curry made with coconut milk should be served over cooked brown rice and topped with fresh cilantro.

Nutrition (per serving):
- Calories: ~350
- Protein: ~10g
- Carbohydrates: ~45g
- Fiber: ~12g
- Fat: ~15g

STUFFED PORTOBELLO MUSHROOMS WITH QUINOA AND SPINACH

Ingredients:

- 4 large Portobello mushrooms, stems removed
- 1 cup cooked quinoa
- 1 cup chopped spinach
- 1/2 cup diced tomatoes
- 1/4 cup diced red onion
- 1/4 cup crumbled feta cheese
- 2 tablespoons olive oil
- 1 tablespoon balsamic vinegar
- Salt and pepper to taste

Instructions:

1. Turn the oven on and set it to 375°F (190°C).
2. On a baking sheet, put the Portobello mushrooms.
3. Cooked quinoa, chopped spinach, tomatoes, red onion, crumbled feta cheese, olive oil, balsamic vinegar, salt, and pepper are all mixed in a bowl.
4. Fill each Portobello mushroom cap with the quinoa filling.
5. Bake in an oven heated for about 15 to 20 minutes or until the mushrooms are soft and the sauce is hot.
6. As a filling and tasty meal, serve the stuffed Portobello mushrooms with rice and spinach.

Nutrition (per serving, one stuffed mushroom):

- Calories: ~250
- Protein: ~10g
- Carbohydrates: ~30g
- Fiber: ~8g
- Fat: ~12g

HIGH-FIBER CRANBERRY WALNUT MUFFINS

Ingredients:

- 1 1/2 cups whole wheat flour
- 1/2 cup oat bran
- 1/4 cup ground flaxseed
- 1/2 cup chopped walnuts
- 1/2 cup dried cranberries
- 1/4 cup honey or maple syrup
- 1 cup unsweetened applesauce
- 1/2 cup almond milk (or any milk of choice)
- 1 egg
- 1 teaspoon vanilla extract
- 1 teaspoon baking powder
- 1/2 teaspoon baking soda
- 1/2 teaspoon ground cinnamon
- Pinch of salt

Instructions:

1. Turn the oven on and set it to 375°F (190°C). Use paper cups to line a muffin pan.
2. Mix the whole wheat flour, oat bran, ground flaxseed, chopped walnuts, dried cranberries, baking powder, baking soda, ground cinnamon, and salt in a large bowl.
3. Mix honey or maple syrup, applesauce that has yet to be sweetened, almond milk, an egg, and vanilla extract in another bowl.
4. Pour the wet ingredients into the dry ingredients and stir until just mixed.
5. Divide the batter between the muffin cups so each is about 3/4 full.

6. Bake for about 18 to 20 minutes or until a toothpick stuck in the middle comes out clean.
7. Let the muffins cool down before you serve them.

Nutrition (per muffin, recipe makes about 12 muffins):

- Calories: ~200
- Protein: ~6g
- Carbohydrates: ~30g
- Fiber: ~8g
- Fat: ~8g

GREEK QUINOA STUFFED TOMATOES

Ingredients:

- 4 large ripe tomatoes
- 1 cup cooked quinoa
- 1/2 cup crumbled feta cheese
- 1/4 cup chopped Kalamata olives
- 1/4 cup diced red onion
- 1/4 cup chopped fresh parsley
- 2 tablespoons olive oil
- 1 tablespoon balsamic vinegar
- 1 teaspoon dried oregano
- Salt and pepper to taste

Instructions:

1. Turn the oven on and set it to 375°F (190°C).
2. Cut the tops off the tomatoes and carefully scoop out the insides, leaving a shell.

3. Mix the cooked quinoa, crumbled feta cheese, chopped Kalamata olives, diced red onion, chopped fresh parsley, olive oil, balsamic vinegar, dried oregano, salt, and pepper in a bowl.
4. Fill each tomato shell with the quinoa filling.
5. Put the tomatoes that have been put in a baking dish.
6. Bake in an oven that has been warm for about 15 to 20 minutes or until the tomatoes are soft and the filling is hot.
7. The Greek quinoa-stuffed tomatoes are a tasty and healthy dish to serve.

Nutrition (per stuffed tomato):

- Calories: ~250
- Protein: ~8g
- Carbohydrates: ~30g
- Fiber: ~8g
- Fat: ~12g

MANGO AND CHIA SEED YOGURT PARFAIT

Ingredients:

- 1 cup Greek yoghurt (plain or vanilla)
- 1 ripe mango, diced
- 2 tablespoons chia seeds
- 1/4 cup granola
- Honey or maple syrup for drizzling

Instructions:

1. Stack Greek yoghurt, diced mango, chia seeds, and granola in a glass or jar.
2. Honey or maple syrup can be used to add more sweetness.
3. As many times as you want.
4. Serve the yoghurt parfait with fruit and chia seeds as a healthy and tasty breakfast or snack.

Nutrition (per parfait):

- Calories: ~300
- Protein: ~15g
- Carbohydrates: ~40g
- Fiber: ~8g
- Fat: ~10g

WHOLE WHEAT VEGGIE AND HUMMUS WRAP

Ingredients:

- 1 large whole wheat tortilla
- 1/4 cup hummus
- 1/2 cup mixed vegetables (bell peppers, cucumber, carrot, etc.)
- Handful of baby spinach leaves
- 2 tablespoons crumbled feta cheese
- Salt and pepper to taste

Instructions:

1. Put the whole wheat tortilla on a clean surface and spread it flat.

2. The hummus was spread on the bread.
3. Mixed veggies, baby spinach leaves, crumbled feta cheese, salt, and pepper are layered on each other.
4. Fold the tortilla's sides in, then roll it up tightly from the bottom.
5. The wrap should be cut in half and served.

Nutrition (per wrap):

- Calories: ~300
- Protein: ~10g
- Carbohydrates: ~40g
- Fiber: ~10g
- Fat: ~10g

FIBER-PACKED PUMPKIN SPICE PANCAKES

Ingredients:

- 1 cup whole wheat flour
- 1/4 cup ground flaxseed
- 1 teaspoon baking powder
- 1/2 teaspoon baking soda
- 1 teaspoon pumpkin pie spice
- 1/4 teaspoon salt
- 1/2 cup pumpkin puree
- 1 cup buttermilk or milk of choice
- 1 egg
- 2 tablespoons maple syrup
- 1 teaspoon vanilla extract

Instructions:

1. Mix the whole wheat flour, ground flaxseed, baking powder, baking soda, pumpkin pie spice, and salt in a big bowl with a whisk.
2. Mix pumpkin puree, buttermilk, an egg, maple syrup, and vanilla extract in another bowl.
3. Pour the wet ingredients into the dry ingredients and stir until just mixed.
4. Heat a pan or grill that doesn't stick to medium heat.
5. For each pancake, pour 1/4 cup of batter into the pan.
6. Cook until bubbles appear on the top, then flip and cook for 1-2 minutes.
7. Serve the pancakes with a drizzle of maple syrup. The pancakes are full of grain and pumpkin spice.

Nutrition (per pancake, recipe makes about 8 pancakes):

- Calories: ~200
- Protein: ~8g
- Carbohydrates: ~30g
- Fiber: ~8g
- Fat: ~6g

LENTIL AND SWEET POTATO STEW

Ingredients:

- 1 cup dried green or brown lentils, soaked and cooked (or 1 can of lentils, drained and rinsed)
- 2 cups diced sweet potatoes
- 1 onion, chopped
- 2 cloves garlic, minced

- 1 can (14 oz) diced tomatoes
- 4 cups vegetable broth
- 1 teaspoon ground cumin
- 1/2 teaspoon ground cinnamon
- 1/4 teaspoon cayenne pepper (adjust to taste)
- 2 tablespoons olive oil
- Salt and pepper to taste
- Chopped fresh cilantro for garnish

Instructions:

1. Olive oil is heated over medium heat in a big pot.
2. Cook the onion until it becomes clear.
3. Mix in chopped garlic, cumin powder, cinnamon powder, and cayenne pepper. Cook for about a minute or until the smell is pleasant.
4. Put diced sweet potatoes, already cooked lentils, diced tomatoes, and veggie broth in the pot.
5. Bring the stew to a boil, boil the heat, and cook for about 20 to 25 minutes or until the sweet potatoes are soft.
6. Add salt and pepper to taste.
7. Add chopped fresh cilantro to the lentil and sweet potato stew before you serve it.

Nutrition (per serving):

- Calories: ~300
- Protein: ~12g
- Carbohydrates: ~45g
- Fiber: ~10g
- Fat: ~8g

QUINOA AND SPINACH STUFFED BELL PEPPERS

Ingredients:

- 4 large bell peppers, any colour
- 1 cup cooked quinoa
- 1 cup chopped spinach
- 1/2 cup diced tomatoes
- 1/4 cup diced red onion
- 1/4 cup crumbled feta cheese
- 2 tablespoons olive oil
- 1 teaspoon dried oregano
- Salt and pepper to taste

Instructions:

1. Turn the oven on and set it to 375°F (190°C).
2. Remove the seeds and skins from the bell peppers and cut off the tops.
3. Cooked quinoa, chopped spinach, tomatoes, red onion, crumbled feta cheese, olive oil, dried oregano, salt, and pepper are all mixed in a bowl.
4. Fill each bell pepper with the quinoa filling.
5. Put the bell peppers stuffed in a baking dish and cover them with aluminium foil.
6. Bake for about 25 to 30 minutes in an oven that has already been warm or until the peppers are soft.
7. Take off the paper and bake for another 5 minutes to give the tops a light brown colour.
8. The bell peppers stuffed with quinoa and spinach are a healthy and tasty.

Nutrition (per stuffed pepper):

- Calories: ~250
- Protein: ~10g
- Carbohydrates: ~40g
- Fiber: ~10g
- Fat: ~10g

BLACK BEAN AND CORN ENCHILADAS

Ingredients:

- Eight whole wheat tortillas
- 2 cups cooked black beans
- 1 cup corn kernels (fresh, frozen, or canned)
- 1 cup diced bell peppers (any colour)
- 1/2 cup diced red onion
- One teaspoon of ground cumin
- 1/2 teaspoon chilli powder
- 1/4 teaspoon garlic powder
- 1 1/2 cups enchilada sauce
- 1 cup shredded cheddar or Mexican cheese blend
- Chopped fresh cilantro for garnish
- Sour cream or Greek yoghurt for serving (optional)

Instructions:

1. Turn the oven on and set it to 375°F (190°C). Grease a pan for baking.
2. Mix cooked black beans, corn kernels, diced bell peppers, chopped red onion, ground cumin, chilli powder, and garlic powder in a bowl.
3. To make the whole wheat tortillas easier to roll, heat them slightly.

4. Put a spoonful of the black bean filling on each tortilla, then tightly roll it up.
5. Put the seam side of the rolled tortillas down in the baking dish.
6. Spread the enchilada sauce evenly over the enchiladas.
7. Shred some cheese and put it on top.
8. Bake in an oven that has already been warm for 20 to 25 minutes or until the cheese is melted and bubbly.
9. Serve with sour cream or Greek yoghurt, if you like, and top with chopped fresh cilantro.

Nutrition (per enchilada, recipe makes about eight enchiladas):

- Calories: ~300
- Protein: ~12g
- Carbohydrates: ~40g
- Fiber: ~10g
- Fat: ~10g

HIGH-FIBER APPLE CINNAMON OATMEAL

Ingredients:

- 1 cup old-fashioned oats
- 2 cups water or milk of choice
- 1 apple, diced
- 1/4 cup chopped walnuts
- 1 tablespoon chia seeds
- 1 teaspoon ground cinnamon
- 1 tablespoon honey or maple syrup

Instructions:

1. Bring water or milk to a boil in a pot.
2. Mix in old-fashioned oats and diced apples.
3. Turn down the heat and let the oatmeal simmer, turning now and then, for about 5 to 7 minutes, until the oats are cooked and the apple is soft.
4. Add chopped walnuts, chia seeds, cinnamon powder, honey or maple syrup, and stir.
5. The high-fibre apple cinnamon oatmeal should be served hot.

Nutrition (per serving):

- Calories: ~300
- Protein: ~8g
- Carbohydrates: ~45g
- Fiber: ~10g
- Fat: ~10g

THREE-BEAN AND QUINOA CHILI

Ingredients:

- 1 cup cooked quinoa
- 1 can (15 oz) black beans, drained and rinsed
- 1 can (15 oz) kidney beans, drained and rinsed
- 1 can (15 oz) pinto beans, drained and rinsed
- 1 can (14 oz) diced tomatoes
- 1 cup diced bell peppers (any colour)
- 1 cup diced onion
- 2 cloves garlic, minced
- 1 tablespoon olive oil

- 2 tablespoons chili powder
- 1 teaspoon ground cumin
- 1/2 teaspoon paprika
- 1/4 teaspoon cayenne pepper (adjust to taste)
- Salt and pepper to taste
- Chopped fresh cilantro for garnish

Instructions:

1. Olive oil is heated over medium heat in a big pot.
2. Cook the onion until it becomes clear.
3. Mix in crushed garlic, chilli powder, ground cumin, paprika, and cayenne pepper. Cook for about a minute or until the smell is pleasant.
4. Add tomatoes, bell peppers, cooked rice, black beans, kidney beans, and pinto beans to the pot.
5. Add salt and pepper to taste.
6. Bring the chilli to a boil and cook for 20–25 minutes to let the flavours mix.
7. Cut some fresh cilantro and sprinkle it on the three-bean and quinoa soup.

Nutrition (per serving):

- Calories: ~350
- Protein: ~15g
- Carbohydrates: ~60g
- Fiber: ~15g
- Fat: ~6g

ROASTED RED PEPPER AND HUMMUS SANDWICH

Ingredients:

- 2 slices whole wheat bread
- 1/4 cup hummus
- 1/4 cup roasted red pepper strips
- Handful of baby spinach leaves
- 1/4 avocado, sliced
- Salt and pepper to taste

Instructions:

1. On one side of each slice of whole wheat bread, spread hummus.
2. Stack strips of roasted red pepper, baby spinach leaves, sliced avocado, salt, and pepper.
3. Make a sandwich by putting the other slice of bread on top.
4. The sandwich should be cut in half and served.

Nutrition (per sandwich):

- Calories: ~300
- Protein: ~10g
- Carbohydrates: ~40g
- Fiber: ~10g
- Fat: ~12g

FIBER-RICH MIXED BERRY SMOOTHIE

Ingredients:

- 1 cup mixed berries (blueberries, raspberries, strawberries)
- 1 banana
- 1 cup almond milk (or any milk of choice)
- 1 tablespoon chia seeds
- 1 tablespoon ground flaxseed
- 1/2 cup Greek yoghurt (plain or vanilla)
- Honey or maple syrup for sweetness (optional)

Instructions:

1. Mix the berries, banana, almond milk, chia seeds, ground flaxseed, Greek yoghurt, and honey or maple syrup, if you want, in a blender.
2. Mix until it's creamy and smooth.
3. Pour the drink made with mixed berries into a glass and enjoy.

Nutrition (per smoothie):

- Calories: ~250
- Protein: ~8g
- Carbohydrates: ~40g
- Fiber: ~10g
- Fat: ~8g

THAI COCONUT LENTIL SOUP

Ingredients:

- 1 cup dried red lentils, rinsed and drained
- 1 can (14 oz) coconut milk
- 4 cups vegetable broth
- 1 cup diced bell peppers (any colour)
- 1 cup diced carrots
- 1 cup diced onion
- 2 cloves garlic, minced
- 1 tablespoon Thai red curry paste
- 1 teaspoon grated ginger
- 1 teaspoon ground turmeric
- Juice of 1 lime
- 2 tablespoons chopped fresh cilantro
- Salt and pepper to taste

Instructions:

1. Some vegetable broth should be heated over medium heat in a big pot.
2. Cook the onion until it becomes clear.
3. Add chopped garlic, Thai red curry paste, diced ginger, and ground turmeric. Cook for about a minute or until the smell is pleasant.
4. Dice up some bell peppers and carrots and put them in the pot. Stir and let it cook for a few minutes.
5. Red lentils, coconut milk, and veggie broth should be added. Get the soup boiling.
6. Turn down the heat and let the soup simmer for about 20 to 25 minutes, or until the lentils and veggies are soft.
7. Add lime juice, fresh cilantro that has been chopped, salt, and pepper.
8. Serve the Thai coconut lentil soup as a food that will warm you up and taste great.

Nutrition (per serving):

- Calories: ~300
- Protein: ~15g
- Carbohydrates: ~40g
- Fiber: ~12g
- Fat: ~10g

STUFFED ZUCCHINI WITH QUINOA AND PESTO

Ingredients:

- 2 medium zucchinis
- 1 cup cooked quinoa
- 1/4 cup pesto sauce
- 1/4 cup cherry tomatoes, halved
- 1/4 cup crumbled feta cheese
- Salt and pepper to taste

Instructions:

1. Turn the oven on and set it to 375°F (190°C).
2. Half the zucchinis lengthwise and scoop out the middle to make a hole.
3. Cooked rice, pesto sauce, cherry tomatoes, crumbled feta cheese, salt, and pepper are all mixed in a bowl.
4. Put some of the rice mixture in each half of a zucchini.
5. Put the zucchinis that have been filled on a baking sheet.
6. Bake for about 15 to 20 minutes in an oven that has already been warm or until the zucchinis are soft.
7. As a healthy and tasty meal, serve the stuffed zucchini with rice and pesto.

Nutrition (per serving, one stuffed zucchini half):

- Calories: ~200
- Protein: ~7g
- Carbohydrates: ~20g
- Fiber: ~4g
- Fat: ~10g

HIGH-FIBER PEANUT BUTTER BANANA WAFFLES

Ingredients:

- 1 cup whole wheat flour
- 1/4 cup ground flaxseed
- 1 tablespoon baking powder
- 1/2 teaspoon ground cinnamon
- 1 ripe banana, mashed
- 1/4 cup natural peanut butter
- 1 cup almond milk (or any milk of choice)
- 1 egg
- 1 teaspoon vanilla extract

Instructions:

1. Follow the steps that came with your waffle iron to heat it.
2. Mix whole wheat flour, ground flaxseed, baking powder, and ground cinnamon in a big bowl with a whisk.
3. Mix mashed banana, peanut butter, almond milk, an egg, and vanilla extract in another bowl.

4. Pour the wet ingredients into the dry ingredients and stir until just mixed.
5. Grease the waffle maker a little bit and pour batter on it.
6. Follow the directions on the waffle iron to make waffles.
7. The high-fibre peanut butter banana waffles can be topped with whatever you like.

Nutrition (per waffle, recipe makes about four waffles):
- Calories: ~300
- Protein: ~10g
- Carbohydrates: ~35g
- Fiber: ~8g
- Fat: ~14g

MEDITERRANEAN QUINOA STUFFED PEPPERS

Ingredients:
- 4 large bell peppers, any colour
- 1 cup cooked quinoa
- 1/2 cup diced cucumber
- 1/2 cup diced tomatoes
- 1/4 cup diced red onion
- 1/4 cup crumbled feta cheese
- 2 tablespoons chopped Kalamata olives
- 2 tablespoons chopped fresh parsley
- 1 tablespoon olive oil
- 1 tablespoon balsamic vinegar
- Salt and pepper to taste

Instructions:

1. Turn the oven on and set it to 375°F (190°C).
2. Remove the seeds and skins from the bell peppers and cut off the tops.
3. Mix cooked quinoa, diced cucumber, tomatoes, red onion, crumbled feta cheese, chopped Kalamata olives, chopped fresh parsley, olive oil, balsamic vinegar, salt, and pepper in a bowl.
4. Fill each bell pepper with the quinoa filling.
5. Put the bell peppers stuffed in a baking dish and cover them with aluminium foil.
6. Bake for about 25 to 30 minutes in an oven that has already been warm or until the peppers are soft.
7. Take off the paper and bake for another 5 minutes to give the tops a light brown colour.
8. The Mediterranean stuffed peppers with quinoa are a tasty and healthy dish.

Nutrition (per stuffed pepper):

- Calories: ~250
- Protein: ~8g
- Carbohydrates: ~35g
- Fiber: ~8g
- Fat: ~10g

MIXED BERRY CHIA SEED BREAKFAST BOWL

Ingredients:

- 1/2 cup mixed berries (blueberries, raspberries, strawberries)
- 1/2 cup Greek yoghurt (plain or vanilla)
- 2 tablespoons chia seeds
- 1 tablespoon honey or maple syrup
- 1/4 cup granola
- Sliced almonds for topping (optional)

Instructions:

1. Half of the mixed berries should be mashed with a fork in a bowl to get their juices out.
2. Add Greek yoghurt and chia seeds and mix well.
3. Honey or maple syrup can be drizzled over the mixture and stirred well.
4. Put the mixture in the fridge for at least an hour or overnight so the chia seeds can grow and make the mixture thicker.
5. Before serving it, put the remaining mixed berries, granola, and sliced nuts on top of the chia seed mixture.

Nutrition (per serving):

- Calories: ~300
- Protein: ~10g
- Carbohydrates: ~40g
- Fiber: ~10g
- Fat: ~10g

SPAGHETTI SQUASH WITH LENTIL CURRY

Ingredients:

- 1 medium spaghetti squash
- 1 cup cooked green or brown lentils
- 1 cup coconut milk
- 1 tablespoon curry powder
- 1/2 teaspoon ground turmeric
- 1/2 teaspoon ground cumin
- 1/4 teaspoon cayenne pepper (adjust to taste)
- 1 tablespoon olive oil
- 1 onion, chopped
- 2 cloves garlic, minced
- Salt and pepper to taste
- Chopped fresh cilantro for garnish

Instructions:

1. Turn the oven on and set it to 375°F (190°C).
2. Split the spaghetti squash in half lengthwise and scoop out the seeds.
3. Place the squash halves, cut side down, on a baking sheet. Roast in a warm oven for 30 to 40 minutes or until the squash strands are soft and can be pulled apart with a fork.
4. Make the lentil soup while the squash is in the oven. Olive oil is heated over medium heat in a large pot.
5. Cook the onion until it becomes clear.
6. Mix in the chopped garlic, curry powder, turmeric powder, cumin powder, and cayenne pepper. Cook for about a minute or until the smell is pleasant.
7. Add beans that have been cooked and coconut milk. Allow the scents to mix for about 10 to 15 minutes. You can add a little water if the blend gets too thick.
8. Add salt and pepper to taste.

9. When the spaghetti squash is done cooking, scrape the squash strands into a bowl with a fork.
10. Serve the spaghetti squash with the lentil sauce on top and chopped fresh cilantro on the side as a garnish.

Nutrition (per serving):

- Calories: ~350
- Protein: ~12g
- Carbohydrates: ~45g
- Fiber: ~10g
- Fat: ~15g

ROASTED VEGETABLE AND HUMMUS PANINI

Ingredients:

- 2 slices whole wheat bread
- 2 tablespoons hummus
- 1/4 cup roasted vegetables (bell peppers, zucchini, eggplant, etc.)
- Handful of baby spinach leaves
- 1 slice provolone cheese (or cheese of choice)
- Olive oil or cooking spray

Instructions:

1. Put a sandwich press or a skillet on medium heat to warm up.
2. On one side of each slice of whole wheat bread, spread hummus.

3. Stack roasted veggies, baby spinach leaves, provolone cheese, and the other slice of bread.
4. Brush a little olive oil or cooking spray on the outside of the sandwich.
5. Put the sandwich in the panini press or oven and cook it until the bread is toasted and the cheese is melted.
6. The sandwich should be cut in half and served.

Nutrition (per panini):

- Calories: ~300
- Protein: ~10g
- Carbohydrates: ~40g
- Fiber: ~8g
- Fat: ~10g

FIBER-PACKED CHOCOLATE PROTEIN BARS

Ingredients:

- 1 cup rolled oats
- 1/2 cup chocolate protein powder
- 1/4 cup ground flaxseed
- 1/4 cup chopped nuts (almonds, walnuts, etc.)
- 1/4 cup natural peanut butter
- 1/4 cup honey or maple syrup
- 1/4 cup unsweetened almond milk (or any milk of choice)
- 1/4 cup dark chocolate chips

Instructions:

1. Mix rolled oats, chocolate protein powder, ground flaxseed, and chopped nuts in a big bowl.
2. In a small pot, melt the peanut butter, honey or maple syrup, and almond milk over low heat.
3. Pour the wet mixture into the dry mixture and stir until everything is evenly covered.
4. Add dark chocolate chips and stir.
5. Spread the mixture out with a spoon in a baking dish that has been lined.
6. Put the bars in the fridge for at least 2 hours to set.
7. Make bars from the blend and enjoy.

Nutrition (per bar, recipe makes about 8 bars):
- Calories: ~250
- Protein: ~10g
- Carbohydrates: ~25g
- Fiber: ~6g
- Fat: ~14g

LENTIL AND VEGETABLE STIR-FRY WITH GINGER SOY SAUCE

Ingredients:
- 1 cup cooked green or brown lentils
- 2 cups mixed vegetables (broccoli, bell peppers, carrots, snap peas, etc.)
- 2 cloves garlic, minced
- 1 teaspoon grated ginger
- 2 tablespoons low-sodium soy sauce
- 1 tablespoon hoisin sauce

- 1 tablespoon sesame oil
- 1 tablespoon olive oil
- 2 green onions, sliced
- Sesame seeds for garnish

Instructions:

1. Olive oil should be heated in a wok or a big skillet over medium-high heat.
2. Chop some garlic and grate some ginger. Stir-fry for about a minute until the food smells good.
3. Add the mixed veggies and cook for a few minutes until they soften.
4. Stir in the cooked beans and cook for another two to three minutes.
5. Mix low-sodium soy sauce, hoisin sauce, and sesame oil in a small bowl with a whisk.
6. Pour the sauce over the lentils and vegetables and stir to thoroughly cover them.
7. Cook for another two to three minutes or until everything is hot.
8. Take it off the heat and add sliced green onions.
9. Serve the lentil and vegetable stir-fry over cooked brown rice or quinoa and top with sesame seeds.

Nutrition (per serving):

- Calories: ~300
- Protein: ~15g
- Carbohydrates: ~40g
- Fiber: ~10g
- Fat: ~10g

BLACK BEAN AND SWEET POTATO QUESADILLAS

Ingredients:

- 4 whole wheat tortillas
- 1 cup cooked black beans
- 1 cup cooked sweet potatoes, mashed
- 1/2 cup diced red onion
- 1/2 cup diced bell peppers (any colour)
- 1 teaspoon ground cumin
- 1/2 teaspoon chilli powder
- 1/4 teaspoon garlic powder
- 1 cup shredded cheddar or Mexican cheese blend
- Olive oil or cooking spray

Instructions:

1. Cooked black beans, mashed sweet potatoes, diced red onion, chopped bell peppers, ground cumin, chilli powder, and garlic powder are all mixed in a bowl.
2. Warm up a pan over medium heat.
3. Grease one side of a whole wheat tortilla with oil and put it in the pan with the greased side down.
4. Spread half of the tortilla with the black bean and sweet potato filling.
5. Shred some cheese and sprinkle it on top.
6. To make a half-moon form, fold the other half of the tortilla over the filling.
7. Cook the quesadilla for a few minutes on each side until the cheese is melted and the bread is golden brown.
8. Do the same thing with the rest of the tortillas and filling.
9. Serve the quesadillas by cutting them into wedges.

Nutrition (per quesadilla):

- Calories: ~350
- Protein: ~15g
- Carbohydrates: ~45g
- Fiber: ~10g
- Fat: ~12g

CAPRESE STUFFED PORTOBELLO MUSHROOMS

Ingredients:

- 4 large Portobello mushrooms, stems removed
- 1 cup cherry tomatoes, halved
- 1/2 cup fresh mozzarella cheese, diced
- 1/4 cup chopped fresh basil
- 2 tablespoons balsamic vinegar
- 2 tablespoons olive oil
- Salt and pepper to taste

Instructions:

1. Turn the oven on and set it to 375°F (190°C).
2. On a baking sheet, put the Portobello mushrooms.
3. Mix cherry tomatoes, fresh mozzarella cheese, fresh basil that has been chopped, balsamic vinegar, olive oil, salt, and pepper in a bowl.
4. Fill each Portobello mushroom with the tomato and mozzarella filling.

5. Bake in an oven that has been warm for about 15 to 20 minutes or until the cheese is melted and the mushrooms are soft.
6. Serve the Portobello mushrooms stuffed with Caprese as a tasty and filling dish.

Nutrition (per mushroom):

- Calories: ~200
- Protein: ~10g
- Carbohydrates: ~10g
- Fiber: ~2g
- Fat: ~15g

MANGO AND CHIA SEED SMOOTHIE BOWL

Ingredients:

- 1 ripe mango, diced
- 1 banana
- 1/2 cup unsweetened almond milk (or any milk of choice)
- 2 tablespoons chia seeds
- Toppings: sliced banana, diced mango, shredded coconut, chopped nuts

Instructions:

1. Diced mango, banana, almond milk, and chia seeds should all be put into a mixer.
2. Mix until it's creamy and smooth.
3. The drink should go into a bowl.

4. Banana slices, mango cubes, crushed coconut, and chopped nuts go on top.
5. Use a spoon to eat the mango and chia seed smoothie bowl.

Nutrition (per bowl):

- Calories: ~300
- Protein: ~6g
- Carbohydrates: ~55g
- Fiber: ~10g
- Fat: ~8g

HIGH FIBER ALMOND BUTTER PANCAKES

Ingredients:

- 1 cup whole wheat flour
- 1/4 cup ground flaxseed
- 1 tablespoon baking powder
- 1/2 teaspoon ground cinnamon
- 1 cup almond milk (or any milk of choice)
- 1/4 cup natural almond butter
- 2 tablespoons honey or maple syrup
- 1 teaspoon vanilla extract

Instructions:

1. Put a pan or grill over medium heat to warm up.
2. Mix whole wheat flour, ground flaxseed, baking powder, and ground cinnamon in a big bowl with a whisk.

3. Mix almond milk, almond butter, honey or maple syrup, and vanilla extract in a different bowl until well blended.
4. Pour the wet ingredients into the dry ingredients and stir until just mixed.
5. Grease the pan or grill lightly.
6. Put pancakes on the pan by pouring pancake batter on it.
7. Cook until bubbles appear on the top, then flip and cook until golden brown on the other side.
8. Repeat the steps with the rest of the batter.
9. The high-fibre almond butter pancakes can be topped with anything you like.

Nutrition (per pancake, recipe makes about eight pancakes):

- Calories: ~150
- Protein: ~5g
- Carbohydrates: ~20g
- Fiber: ~4g
- Fat: ~6g

MEXICAN CHICKPEA AND VEGETABLE SOUP

Ingredients:

- 1 can (15 oz) chickpeas, drained and rinsed
- 1 cup diced bell peppers (any colour)
- 1 cup diced zucchini
- 1 cup corn kernels (fresh, frozen, or canned)
- 1 cup diced onion
- 2 cloves garlic, minced

- 1 can (14 oz) diced tomatoes
- 4 cups vegetable broth
- 1 teaspoon ground cumin
- 1/2 teaspoon chilli powder
- 1/4 teaspoon smoked paprika
- Juice of 1 lime
- Chopped fresh cilantro for garnish
- Salt and pepper to taste

Instructions:

1. Olive oil is heated over medium heat in a big pot.
2. Cook the onion until it becomes clear.
3. Add chopped garlic, ground cumin, chilli powder, and smoked paprika. Cook for about a minute or until the smell is pleasant.
4. Add diced bell peppers, zucchini, corn kernels, tomatoes, chickpeas, and veggie broth to the pot.
5. Add salt and pepper to taste.
6. Bring the soup to a boil, turn down the heat and let it cook for 20–25 minutes to let the flavours mix.
7. Add chopped fresh cilantro and lime juice.
8. Serve the hearty and tasty Mexican chickpea and veggie soup.

Nutrition (per serving):

- Calories: ~250
- Protein: ~10g
- Carbohydrates: ~45g
- Fiber: ~10g
- Fat: ~4g

QUINOA AND BLACK BEAN STUFFED BELL PEPPERS

Ingredients:

- 4 large bell peppers, any colour
- 1 cup cooked quinoa
- 1 can (15 oz) black beans, drained and rinsed
- 1 cup corn kernels (fresh, frozen, or canned)
- 1 cup diced tomatoes
- 1/2 cup diced red onion
- 1 teaspoon ground cumin
- 1/2 teaspoon chilli powder
- 1/4 teaspoon garlic powder
- 1 cup shredded cheddar or Mexican cheese blend
- Chopped fresh cilantro for garnish

Instructions:

1. Turn the oven on and set it to 375°F (190°C).
2. Remove the seeds and skins from the bell peppers and cut off the tops.
3. Cooked quinoa, black beans, corn kernels, diced tomatoes, diced red onion, ground cumin, chilli powder, and garlic powder are all mixed together in a bowl.
4. Fill each bell pepper with the rice and black bean mixture.
5. Put the bell peppers stuffed in a baking dish and cover them with aluminium foil.
6. Bake for about 25 to 30 minutes in an oven that has already been warm or until the peppers are soft.
7. Take off the paper and top each stuffed pepper with shredded cheese.
8. Bake for another 5 minutes until the cheese is bubbling and melted.

9. Serve the bell peppers stuffed with rice and black beans as a healthy and filling meal.

Nutrition (per stuffed pepper):

- Calories: ~300
- Protein: ~15g
- Carbohydrates: ~45g
- Fiber: ~10g
- Fat: ~10g

FIBER-RICH BLUEBERRY OAT BRAN MUFFINS

Ingredients:

- 1 cup oat bran
- 1/2 cup whole wheat flour
- 1/4 cup ground flaxseed
- 1/4 cup brown sugar or coconut sugar
- 1 teaspoon baking powder
- 1/2 teaspoon baking soda
- 1/2 teaspoon ground cinnamon
- 1/2 cup unsweetened applesauce
- 1/4 cup Greek yogurt
- 1/4 cup almond milk (or any milk of choice)
- 1 egg
- 1 teaspoon vanilla extract
- 1 cup blueberries (fresh or frozen)

Instructions:

1. Turn the oven on and set it to 375°F (190°C). Use paper cups to line a muffin pan.
2. Mix oat bran, whole wheat flour, ground flaxseed, brown sugar, baking powder, baking soda, and ground cinnamon in a big bowl with a whisk.
3. Combine the applesauce, Greek yoghurt, almond milk, egg, and vanilla extract in a different bowl.
4. Pour the wet ingredients into the dry ingredients and stir until just mixed.
5. Gently add the blueberries.
6. Fill each muffin cup about two-thirds of the way with the batter.
7. Bake in an oven that has already been heated for about 15 to 20 minutes or until a knife stuck into the middle of a muffin comes out clean.
8. Let the muffins cool for a few minutes in the pan before moving them to a wire rack to finish cooling.

Nutrition (per muffin, recipe makes about 12 muffins):
- Calories: ~150
- Protein: ~6g
- Carbohydrates: ~25g
- Fiber: ~6g
- Fat: ~4g

RATATOUILLE AND BROWN RICE BOWL

Ingredients:
- 2 cups cooked brown rice

- 1 medium eggplant, diced
- 1 medium zucchini, diced
- 1 bell pepper, diced
- 1 onion, diced
- 2 cloves garlic, minced
- 1 can (14 oz) diced tomatoes
- 2 tablespoons tomato paste
- 1 teaspoon dried thyme
- 1 teaspoon dried oregano
- 1/2 teaspoon dried basil
- Salt and pepper to taste
- Olive oil for cooking
- Fresh basil leaves for garnish

Instructions:

1. Olive oil is heated over medium heat in a large pot.
2. Add chopped bell pepper and onion. Cook them until they begin to get soft.
3. Add the minced garlic and cook for another minute.
4. Mix in the eggplant and zucchini pieces. Please wait a few minutes until they start to turn brown.
5. Add chopped tomatoes, tomato paste, dried thyme, dried oregano, dried basil, salt, and pepper. Stir to mix.
6. Cover the skillet and let the mixture simmer for 15 to 20 minutes, or until the veggies are soft and the flavours are well developed.
7. Put the ratatouille on top of cooked brown rice and add fresh basil leaves for decoration.

Nutrition (per serving):

- Calories: ~300
- Protein: ~6g
- Carbohydrates: ~60g

- Fiber: ~10g
- Fat: ~4g

THREE-BEAN AND BARLEY CHILI

Ingredients:

- 1 cup cooked barley
- 1 can (15 oz) black beans, drained and rinsed
- 1 can (15 oz) kidney beans, drained and rinsed
- 1 can (15 oz) pinto beans, drained and rinsed
- 1 can (14 oz) diced tomatoes
- 1 cup vegetable broth
- 1 cup diced bell peppers (any colour)
- 1 cup diced onion
- 2 cloves garlic, minced
- 1 tablespoon chilli powder
- 1 teaspoon ground cumin
- 1/2 teaspoon paprika
- 1/4 teaspoon cayenne pepper (adjust to taste)
- Salt and pepper to taste
- Chopped fresh cilantro for garnish

Instructions:

1. Olive oil is heated over medium heat in a big pot.
2. Cook the onion until it becomes clear.
3. Add the diced bell peppers and cook for a few minutes until they soften.
4. Mix in crushed garlic, chilli powder, ground cumin, paprika, and cayenne pepper. Cook for about a minute or until the smell is pleasant.

5. Mix in cooked barley, black beans, kidney beans, pinto beans, diced tomatoes, and veggie broth.
6. Add salt and pepper to taste.
7. Bring the chilli to a boil, turn down the heat and let it cook for about 15 to 20 minutes to let the flavours mix.
8. The chopped fresh cilantro goes well with the three-bean and barley soup.

Nutrition (per serving):

- Calories: ~350
- Protein: ~15g
- Carbohydrates: ~60g
- Fiber: ~15g
- Fat: ~2g

ROASTED RED PEPPER AND HUMMUS WRAP

Ingredients:

- 1 large whole wheat tortilla
- 1/4 cup hummus
- 1/4 cup roasted red pepper strips
- 1/4 cup sliced cucumber
- 1/4 cup sliced red onion
- Handful of mixed greens
- Salt and pepper to taste

Instructions:

1. Put the whole wheat tortilla on a clean surface and spread it flat.

2. Spread hummus on the bread in an even layer.
3. Put pieces of roasted red pepper, cucumber slices, red onion, and mixed greens on one side of the tortilla.
4. Add salt and pepper to taste.
5. To make a wrap, tightly roll up the dough.
6. Cut the wrap in half across the middle to serve.

Nutrition (per wrap):

- Calories: ~250
- Protein: ~8g
- Carbohydrates: ~35g
- Fiber: ~8g
- Fat: ~10g

FIBER-PACKED MIXED BERRY CHIA JAM

Ingredients:

- 2 cups mixed berries (blueberries, raspberries, strawberries)
- 2 tablespoons chia seeds
- 2 tablespoons honey or maple syrup (adjust to taste)
- Juice of 1 lemon

Instructions:

1. Heat mixed berries over medium heat in a skillet until they break down and let out their juices.
2. Use a fork or a potato masher to mash the berries to the desired consistency.
3. Mix in honey or maple syrup, chia seeds, and lemon juice.

4. Keep cooking the mixture for a few more minutes until it thickens.
5. Take the chia jam off the heat and let it cool.
6. Put the chia jam in a glass jar in the fridge until it is set.

Nutrition (per tablespoon):

- Calories: ~20
- Protein: ~<1g
- Carbohydrates: ~5g
- Fiber: ~1g
- Fat: ~<1g

THAI LENTIL AND VEGETABLE STIR-FRY

Ingredients:

- 1 cup cooked green or brown lentils
- 2 cups mixed vegetables (bell peppers, carrots, snap peas, etc.)
- 2 tablespoons low-sodium soy sauce
- 2 tablespoons hoisin sauce
- 1 tablespoon lime juice
- 1 tablespoon olive oil
- 1 teaspoon grated ginger
- 2 cloves garlic, minced
- Crushed red pepper flakes (optional)
- Chopped fresh cilantro for garnish
- Chopped peanuts for garnish (optional)

Instructions:

1. Olive oil should be heated in a wok or a big skillet over medium-high heat.
2. Add chopped garlic, grated ginger, and red pepper flakes that have been crushed. Cook for about a minute or until the smell is pleasant.
3. Add the mixed veggies and cook for a few minutes until they soften.
4. Stir in the cooked beans and cook for another 2–3 minutes.
5. Mix low-sodium soy sauce, hoisin sauce, lime juice, and a splash of water in a small bowl.
6. Pour the sauce over the lentils and vegetables and stir to thoroughly cover them.
7. Cook for another two to three minutes or until everything is hot.
8. Take the dish off the heat and add chopped fresh cilantro.
9. Serve the Thai lentil and vegetable stir-fry over cooked brown rice or quinoa and top with chopped peanuts.

Nutrition (per serving):

- Calories: ~300
- Protein: ~15g
- Carbohydrates: ~45g
- Fiber: ~10g
- Fat: ~6g

STUFFED BELL PEPPERS WITH QUINOA AND SPINACH

Ingredients:

- 4 large bell peppers, any colour

- 1 cup cooked quinoa
- 2 cups baby spinach, chopped
- 1 can (15 oz) black beans, drained and rinsed
- 1 cup diced tomatoes
- 1/2 cup shredded cheddar or Mexican cheese blend
- 1 teaspoon ground cumin
- 1/2 teaspoon chilli powder
- Salt and pepper to taste
- Olive oil for cooking

Instructions:

1. Turn the oven on and set it to 375°F (190°C).
2. Remove the seeds and skins from the bell peppers and cut off the tops.
3. Mix cooked rice, chopped baby spinach, black beans, diced tomatoes, shredded cheese, ground cumin, chilli powder, salt, and pepper in a bowl.
4. Fill each bell pepper with the rice and spinach mixture.
5. Put the bell peppers that have been stuffed in a baking dish.
6. Cover the dish with aluminium foil and bake it in an oven for 25 to 30 minutes or until the peppers are soft.
7. Take off the paper and bake for 5 minutes more to melt the cheese.
8. Serve the stuffed bell peppers as a healthy meal that will fill you up.

Nutrition (per stuffed pepper):

- Calories: ~300
- Protein: ~15g
- Carbohydrates: ~45g
- Fiber: ~12g
- Fat: ~8g

PEACH AND CHIA SEED YOGURT PARFAIT

Ingredients:

- 1 cup Greek yogurt
- 1 ripe peach, diced
- 2 tablespoons chia seeds
- 2 tablespoons granola
- Honey or maple syrup for drizzling

Instructions:

1. Stack Greek yoghurt, diced peach, chia seeds, and granola in a glass or jar.
2. Honey or maple syrup can be used on top.
3. If you want, you can add more layers.
4. Put the dessert in the fridge for at least 30 minutes to let the chia seeds thicken and grow.
5. The peach and chia seed yoghurt dessert is a tasty and healthy way to start or end the day.

Nutrition (per serving):

- Calories: ~300
- Protein: ~15g
- Carbohydrates: ~40g
- Fiber: ~10g
- Fat: ~10g

WHOLE WHEAT VEGGIE BURRITO

Ingredients:

- 1 large whole wheat tortilla
- 1/2 cup cooked brown rice
- 1/2 cup black beans, drained and rinsed
- 1/4 cup diced bell peppers (any colour)
- 1/4 cup diced red onion
- 1/4 cup corn kernels (fresh, frozen, or canned)
- 1/4 cup shredded cheddar or Mexican cheese blend
- 2 tablespoons salsa
- Salt and pepper to taste

Instructions:

1. Put the whole wheat tortilla on a clean surface and spread it flat.
2. Put cooked brown rice, black beans, chopped bell peppers, diced red onion, corn kernels, shredded cheese, and salsa in the middle of the tortilla.
3. Add salt and pepper to taste.
4. Make a burrito by folding in the sides of the dough and rolling it up tightly.
5. The whole wheat veggie taco is a healthy meal that will fill you up.

Nutrition (per burrito):

- Calories: ~350
- Protein: ~15g
- Carbohydrates: ~50g
- Fiber: ~10g
- Fat: ~10g

HIGH-FIBER PUMPKIN SPICE WAFFLES

Ingredients:

- 1 cup whole wheat flour
- 1/2 cup oat flour
- 1/4 cup ground flaxseed
- 1 tablespoon baking powder
- 1 teaspoon pumpkin spice mix
- 1/2 teaspoon cinnamon
- 1 cup canned pumpkin puree
- 1 cup unsweetened almond milk (or any milk of choice)
- 1/4 cup pure maple syrup
- 1 teaspoon vanilla extract

Instructions:

1. Follow the directions on the box to heat a waffle iron.
2. Mix the whole wheat flour, oat flour, ground flaxseed, baking powder, pumpkin spice mix, and cinnamon in a big bowl with a whisk.
3. Combine the pumpkin puree from a can in a different bowl, the almond milk, the maple syrup, and the vanilla extract.
4. Pour the wet ingredients into the dry ingredients and stir until just mixed.
5. Grease the waffle iron lightly and pour the batter in the middle of it.
6. Close the waffle pan and cook it according to the instructions that came with it.
7. Repeat the steps with the rest of the batter.

8. Serve the pumpkin spice waffles with whatever toppings you like.

Nutrition (per waffle, recipe makes about 4 waffles):
- Calories: ~250
- Protein: ~7g
- Carbohydrates: ~45g
- Fiber: ~10g
- Fat: ~5g

MEDITERRANEAN LENTIL AND VEGETABLE SOUP

Ingredients:
- 1 cup cooked green or brown lentils
- 2 cups diced tomatoes
- 1 cup diced bell peppers (any colour)
- 1 cup diced zucchini
- 1 cup diced onion
- 2 cloves garlic, minced
- 4 cups vegetable broth
- 1 teaspoon dried oregano
- 1/2 teaspoon dried thyme
- 1/2 teaspoon dried rosemary
- Salt and pepper to taste
- Olive oil for cooking
- Chopped fresh parsley for garnish

Instructions:

1. Olive oil is heated over medium heat in a big pot.
2. Add chopped bell peppers and onion. Cook the onion until it is clear.
3. Add the minced garlic and cook for another minute.
4. Mix in diced tomatoes and chopped zucchini. Cook for a short time.
5. Add cooked lentils, veggie broth, oregano, thyme, and rosemary that have been dried.
6. Add salt and pepper to taste.
7. Bring the soup to a boil, turn down the heat and let it cook for about 15 to 20 minutes to let the flavours blend.
8. The Mediterranean lentil and veggie soup is a healthy and tasty dish.

Nutrition (per serving):
- Calories: ~250
- Protein: ~15g
- Carbohydrates: ~40g
- Fiber: ~12g
- Fat: ~2g

LENTIL AND SPINACH STUFFED MUSHROOMS

Ingredients:
- 12 large button mushrooms, stems removed
- 1 cup cooked green or brown lentils
- 1 cup chopped baby spinach
- 1/2 cup diced red onion
- 1/4 cup shredded mozzarella cheese

- 2 cloves garlic, minced
- 2 tablespoons olive oil
- 1 tablespoon balsamic vinegar
- Salt and pepper to taste

Instructions:

1. Turn the oven on and set it to 375°F (190°C).
2. The mushroom caps should be put on a baking sheet.
3. Heat olive oil in a pan over medium heat.
4. Add chopped red onion and cook until the onion becomes transparent.
5. Add the minced garlic and cook for another minute.
6. Add the chopped baby spinach and cook until it wilts.
7. Mix the cooked lentils, the spinach mixture, the shredded mozzarella cheese, the balsamic vinegar, the salt, and the pepper in a bowl.
8. Fill each mushroom cap with the lentil and spinach filling.
9. Bake for about 15 to 20 minutes in an oven that has already been warm or until the mushrooms are soft.
10. The mushrooms stuffed with lentils and spinach are a tasty appetizer or side meal.

Nutrition (per serving, serving size is two stuffed mushrooms):

- Calories: ~150
- Protein: ~8g
- Carbohydrates: ~20g
- Fiber: ~6g
- Fat: ~6g

BLACK BEAN AND CORN QUESADILLAS

Ingredients:

- 2 large whole wheat tortillas
- 1 cup canned black beans, drained and rinsed
- 1 cup corn kernels (fresh, frozen, or canned)
- 1/2 cup diced red onion
- 1/2 cup shredded cheddar or Mexican cheese blend
- 1 teaspoon ground cumin
- 1/2 teaspoon chilli powder
- Salt and pepper to taste
- Olive oil for cooking
- Salsa and Greek yoghurt for serving

Instructions:

1. Mix black beans, corn kernels, diced red onion, cumin powder, chilli powder, salt, and pepper in a bowl.
2. Put one whole wheat tortilla on a clean surface and flatten it.
3. On one half of the tortilla, sprinkle half of the shredded cheese.
4. Put the blend of black beans and corn on top of the cheese.
5. Sprinkle the rest of the shreds of cheese on top.
6. Make a half-moon shape by folding the other half of the tortilla over the centre.
7. Do the same thing with the second tortilla.
8. On medium heat, put the olive oil in a pan.
9. Cook each quesadilla for 2 to 3 minutes on each side until the dough is crispy and the cheese is melted.

10. Serve the quesadillas with salsa and Greek yoghurt in pieces.

Nutrition (per quesadilla):

- Calories: ~350
- Protein: ~15g
- Carbohydrates: ~50g
- Fiber: ~10g
- Fat: ~10g

FIBER-RICH BLUEBERRY CHIA SEED OATMEAL

Ingredients:

- 1/2 cup rolled oats
- 1 cup unsweetened almond milk (or any milk of choice)
- 1/2 cup blueberries (fresh or frozen)
- 2 tablespoons chia seeds
- 1 tablespoon honey or maple syrup
- 1/2 teaspoon vanilla extract
- Pinch of salt
- Chopped nuts or additional blueberries for topping

Instructions:

1. Mix rolled oats and almond milk in a pot.
2. Bring to a boil, then turn down the heat to a simmer.
3. To the rice, add blueberries and chia seeds.
4. Keep cooking, stirring now and then, until the oatmeal thickens and the blueberries pop.

5. Take it off the heat and stir in honey or maple syrup, vanilla flavour, and a pinch of salt.
6. Fill a bowl with oatmeal.
7. If you want, you can add chopped nuts or more blueberries on top.
8. Blueberry chia seed cereal is a warm and filling breakfast full of fibre.

Nutrition (per serving):

- Calories: ~300
- Protein: ~7g
- Carbohydrates: ~45g
- Fiber: ~10g
- Fat: ~10g

SPAGHETTI SQUASH WITH CHICKPEA MARINARA

Ingredients:

- 1 medium spaghetti squash
- 1 can (15 oz) chickpeas, drained and rinsed
- 1 can (14 oz) diced tomatoes
- 1/2 cup diced onion
- 2 cloves garlic, minced
- 1 teaspoon dried oregano
- 1/2 teaspoon dried basil
- 1/4 teaspoon red pepper flakes (adjust to taste)
- Salt and pepper to taste
- Olive oil for cooking

- Fresh basil leaves for garnish
- Grated Parmesan cheese for serving (optional)

Instructions:

1. Turn the oven on and set it to 375°F (190°C).
2. Split the spaghetti squash in half lengthwise and scoop out the seeds.
3. Olive oil the cut sides of the squash and put them on a baking sheet with the cut side down.
4. Bake in an oven that has already been heated for about 40 to 45 minutes or until the squash pieces are soft enough to pull apart with a fork.
5. Make the chickpea marinara sauce while the squash is in the oven.
6. Heat olive oil in a pan over medium heat.
7. Cook the onion until it becomes clear.
8. Add the minced garlic and cook for another minute.
9. Mix in diced tomatoes, beans, dried oregano, dried basil, red pepper flakes, salt, and pepper.
10. Allow the sauce to simmer for about 10–15 minutes to blend the flavours.
11. Put the cooked spaghetti squash strands into a bowl with a fork.
12. Chickpea marinara sauce should be served on top of the spaghetti squash.
13. If you want, you can decorate with fresh basil leaves and chopped Parmesan cheese.

Nutrition (per serving):

- Calories: ~300
- Protein: ~12g
- Carbohydrates: ~50g
- Fiber: ~10g

- Fat: ~6g

ROASTED VEGETABLE AND HUMMUS PANINI

Ingredients:

- 2 slices whole wheat bread
- 1/4 cup hummus
- 1/2 cup roasted vegetables (bell peppers, zucchini, eggplant, etc.)
- Handful of baby spinach leaves
- 2 tablespoons shredded mozzarella cheese (optional)
- Olive oil for cooking

Instructions:

1. Spread hummus on one side of each slice of whole wheat bread in an even layer.
2. On one slice of bread, you can layer roasted veggies, baby spinach leaves, and shredded mozzarella cheese if you want to.
3. Make a sandwich by putting the other slice of bread on top.
4. On medium heat, put the olive oil in a pan.
5. Put the sandwich in the pan and cook it until the bread is toasted and the cheese is melting if you're using it.
6. Carefully turn the sandwich over and toast the other side.
7. Cut the sandwich with roasted vegetables and hummus in half to serve.

Nutrition (per panini):

- Calories: ~300
- Protein: ~12g
- Carbohydrates: ~40g
- Fiber: ~8g
- Fat: ~10g

FIBER-PACKED CHOCOLATE AVOCADO BARS

Ingredients:
- 1 cup rolled oats
- 1/2 cup almond flour
- 1/4 cup cocoa powder
- 1/4 teaspoon salt
- 1 ripe avocado, mashed
- 1/2 cup honey or maple syrup
- 1/4 cup unsweetened almond milk (or any milk of choice)
- 1 teaspoon vanilla extract
- 1/4 cup dark chocolate chips

Instructions:
1. Set the oven to 350°F (175°C) and put parchment paper in a baking dish.
2. Mix the rolled oats, almond flour, cocoa powder, and salt in a bowl.
3. Mix the mashed avocado, honey or maple syrup, almond milk, and vanilla extract in a different bowl until smooth.
4. Mix the wet and dry ingredients and stir until everything is mixed well.

5. Add the dark chocolate chips to the mixture.
6. Press the mixture evenly into the baking dish that has been set up.
7. Bake the bars in an oven that has already been warm for 20 to 25 minutes or until they are firm.
8. Let the bars cool down before you cut them into squares.

Nutrition (per bar, recipe makes about 12 bars):

- Calories: ~150
- Protein: ~3g
- Carbohydrates: ~20g
- Fiber: ~4g
- Fat: ~7g

LENTIL AND VEGETABLE STIR-FRY WITH SESAME GINGER SAUCE

Ingredients:

- 1 cup cooked green or brown lentils
- 2 cups mixed vegetables (broccoli, carrots, bell peppers, etc.)
- 2 tablespoons low-sodium soy sauce
- 1 tablespoon sesame oil
- 1 tablespoon rice vinegar
- 1 teaspoon honey or maple syrup
- 1 teaspoon grated ginger
- 2 cloves garlic, minced
- Sesame seeds for garnish

Instructions:

1. Heat sesame oil over medium-high heat in a wok or a big skillet.
2. Chop some garlic and grate some ginger. Cook for about a minute or until the smell is pleasant.
3. Add the mixed veggies and cook for a few minutes until they soften.
4. Stir in the cooked beans and cook for another 2–3 minutes.
5. Mix low-sodium soy sauce, rice vinegar, honey or maple syrup, and a splash of water in a small bowl.
6. Pour the sauce over the lentils and vegetables and stir to thoroughly cover them.
7. Cook for another two to three minutes or until everything is hot.
8. Take it off the heat and sprinkle sesame seeds on top.
9. Serve the bean and vegetable stir-fry over brown rice or quinoa that has already been cooked.

Nutrition (per serving):

- Calories: ~300
- Protein: ~12g
- Carbohydrates: ~45g
- Fiber: ~10g
- Fat: ~8g

QUINOA AND BLACK BEAN STUFFED ZUCCHINI

Ingredients:

- 2 large zucchini

- 1 cup cooked quinoa
- 1 cup canned black beans, drained and rinsed
- 1/2 cup diced bell peppers (any colour)
- 1/2 cup diced red onion
- 1/2 cup corn kernels (fresh, frozen, or canned)
- 1/4 cup shredded cheddar or Mexican cheese blend
- 1 teaspoon ground cumin
- 1/2 teaspoon chilli powder
- Salt and pepper to taste
- Olive oil for cooking

Instructions:

1. Turn the oven on and set it to 375°F (190°C).
2. Cut the zucchini in half lengthwise and scoop out the middle to make a spot that can be filled.
3. Mix cooked quinoa, black beans, diced bell peppers, chopped red onion, corn kernels, shredded cheese, ground cumin, chilli powder, salt, and pepper in a bowl.
4. Put some rice and black bean mix into each half of the zucchini.
5. Put the zucchini that has been stuffed in a baking dish.
6. Cover the dish with aluminium foil and bake it in an oven that has already been warm for 20 to 25 minutes or until the zucchini is soft.
7. Take off the paper and bake for 5 minutes more to melt the cheese.
8. The zucchini stuffed with quinoa and black beans is a healthy and tasty.

Nutrition (per serving, serving size is one stuffed zucchini half):

- Calories: ~250
- Protein: ~10g

- Carbohydrates: ~40g
- Fiber: ~10g
- Fat: ~6g

CAPRESE QUINOA STUFFED BELL PEPPERS

Ingredients:

- 4 large bell peppers, any colour
- 1 cup cooked quinoa
- 1 cup diced tomatoes
- 1/2 cup diced fresh mozzarella cheese
- 1/4 cup chopped fresh basil leaves
- 2 tablespoons balsamic vinegar
- 1 tablespoon olive oil
- Salt and pepper to taste

Instructions:

1. Turn the oven on and set it to 375°F (190°C).
2. Remove the seeds and skins from the bell peppers and cut off the tops.
3. Mix cooked quinoa, diced tomatoes, diced fresh mozzarella cheese, chopped fresh basil leaves, balsamic vinegar, olive oil, salt, and pepper in a bowl.
4. Fill each bell pepper with the quinoa filling.
5. Put the bell peppers that have been stuffed in a baking dish.
6. Cover the dish with aluminium foil and bake it in an oven for 25 to 30 minutes or until the peppers are soft.
7. Take off the paper and bake for 5 minutes more.

8. Serve the bell peppers stuffed with rice and caprese as a tasty and filling dish.

Nutrition (per stuffed pepper):

- Calories: ~300
- Protein: ~12g
- Carbohydrates: ~40g
- Fiber: ~8g
- Fat: ~10g

MANGO AND CHIA SEED BREAKFAST PARFAIT

Ingredients:

- 1 cup Greek yogurt
- 1 ripe mango, diced
- 2 tablespoons chia seeds
- 2 tablespoons granola
- Honey or maple syrup for drizzling

Instructions:

1. Stack Greek yoghurt, diced mango, chia seeds, and granola in a glass or jar.
2. Honey or maple syrup can be used on top.
3. If you want, you can add more layers.
4. Put the dessert in the fridge for at least 30 minutes to let the chia seeds thicken and grow.
5. The mango and chia seed smoothie for breakfast is a healthy and refreshing way to start the day.

Nutrition (per serving):

- Calories: ~300
- Protein: ~15g
- Carbohydrates: ~40g
- Fiber: ~10g
- Fat: ~10g

HIGH-FIBER APPLE WALNUT PANCAKES

Ingredients:

- 1 cup whole wheat flour
- 1/2 cup rolled oats
- 1/4 cup chopped walnuts
- 1 tablespoon ground flaxseed
- 1 tablespoon baking powder
- 1 teaspoon ground cinnamon
- 1/4 teaspoon nutmeg
- 1 cup unsweetened applesauce
- 1 cup unsweetened almond milk (or any milk of choice)
- 1 tablespoon honey or maple syrup
- 1 teaspoon vanilla extract

Instructions:

1. Mix whole wheat flour, rolled oats, chopped walnuts, ground flaxseed, baking powder, cinnamon, and nutmeg in a bowl.
2. Mix raw applesauce, almond milk, honey or maple syrup, and vanilla extract in a separate bowl.

3. Pour the wet ingredients into the dry ingredients and stir until just mixed.
4. Heat a pan or grill that doesn't stick to medium heat.
5. For each pancake, pour about 1/4 cup of batter into the pan.
6. Cook until bubbles are on the top, then flip and cook until both sides are golden brown.
7. Serve the apple walnut pancakes, which are high in fibre, with your favourite toppings.

Nutrition (per pancake, recipe makes about eight pancakes):

- Calories: ~150
- Protein: ~4g
- Carbohydrates: ~25g
- Fiber: ~5g
- Fat: ~5g

MEXICAN CHICKPEA AND VEGETABLE SOUP

Ingredients:

- 1 can (15 oz) chickpeas, drained and rinsed
- 2 cups diced tomatoes
- 1 cup diced bell peppers (any colour)
- 1 cup diced zucchini
- 1 cup diced onion
- 2 cloves garlic, minced
- 4 cups vegetable broth
- 1 teaspoon ground cumin

- 1/2 teaspoon chilli powder
- 1/4 teaspoon smoked paprika
- Salt and pepper to taste
- Olive oil for cooking
- Chopped fresh cilantro for garnish
- Lime wedges for serving

Instructions:

1. Olive oil is heated over medium heat in a big pot.
2. Add chopped bell peppers and onion. Cook the onion until it is clear.
3. Add the minced garlic and cook for another minute.
4. Mix in diced tomatoes and chopped zucchini. Cook for a short time.
5. Add chickpeas, veggie broth, chilli powder, smoked paprika, ground cumin, salt, and pepper.
6. Bring the soup to a boil, boil it, and let it cook for about 15 to 20 minutes.
7. Taste the food and, if necessary, change the spices.
8. Serve the Mexican chickpea and vegetable soup with chopped fresh cilantro and lime wedges on top.

Nutrition (per serving):

- Calories: ~250
- Protein: ~10g
- Carbohydrates: ~40g
- Fiber: ~10g
- Fat: ~4g

QUINOA AND BLACK BEAN STUFFED BELL PEPPERS

Ingredients:

- 4 large bell peppers, any colour
- 1 cup cooked quinoa
- 1 cup canned black beans, drained and rinsed
- 1/2 cup diced tomatoes
- 1/2 cup diced red onion
- 1/4 cup chopped fresh cilantro
- 1 teaspoon ground cumin
- 1/2 teaspoon chilli powder
- Salt and pepper to taste
- Olive oil for cooking

Instructions:

1. Turn the oven on and set it to 375°F (190°C).
2. Remove the seeds and skins from the bell peppers and cut off the tops.
3. Mix cooked rice, black beans, tomatoes, red onion, chopped fresh cilantro, ground cumin, chilli powder, salt, and pepper in a bowl.
4. Fill each bell pepper with the rice and black bean mixture.
5. Put the bell peppers that have been stuffed in a baking dish.
6. Cover the dish with aluminium foil and bake it in an oven for 25 to 30 minutes or until the peppers are soft.
7. Take off the paper and bake for 5 minutes more.
8. The bell peppers stuffed with quinoa and black beans are a tasty and filling.

Nutrition (per stuffed pepper):

- Calories: ~300
- Protein: ~10g
- Carbohydrates: ~45g
- Fiber: ~12g
- Fat: ~6g

FIBER-RICH BLUEBERRY OAT BRAN MUFFINS

Ingredients:
- 1 cup oat bran
- 1/2 cup whole wheat flour
- 1/4 cup ground flaxseed
- 1 teaspoon baking powder
- 1/2 teaspoon baking soda
- 1/2 teaspoon ground cinnamon
- 1/4 teaspoon salt
- 1/2 cup unsweetened applesauce
- 1/4 cup honey or maple syrup
- 1/4 cup unsweetened almond milk (or any milk of choice)
- 1 egg
- 1 teaspoon vanilla extract
- 1 cup blueberries (fresh or frozen)

Instructions:
1. Set the oven to 375°F (190°C) and put paper cups in a muffin pan.

2. Mix oat bran, whole wheat flour, ground flaxseed, baking powder, baking soda, ground cinnamon, and salt in a bowl with a whisk.
3. Mix dry applesauce, honey or maple syrup, almond milk, an egg, and vanilla extract in a separate bowl.
4. Pour the wet ingredients into the dry ingredients and stir until just mixed.
5. Gently add the blueberries.
6. Put the same amount of batter in each muffin cup.
7. Bake in an oven that has already been heated for about 15 to 20 minutes or until a knife stuck into the middle of a muffin comes out clean.
8. Let the muffins cool down before you serve them.

Nutrition (per muffin, recipe makes about 12 muffins):

- Calories: ~150
- Protein: ~4g
- Carbohydrates: ~25g
- Fiber: ~6g
- Fat: ~4g

RATATOUILLE AND BROWN RICE BOWL

Ingredients:

- 2 cups cooked brown rice
- 1 cup diced eggplant
- 1 cup diced zucchini
- 1 cup diced bell peppers (any colour)
- 1 cup diced tomatoes

- 1/2 cup diced onion
- 2 cloves garlic, minced
- 2 tablespoons olive oil
- 1 teaspoon dried thyme
- 1 teaspoon dried oregano
- Salt and pepper to taste
- Chopped fresh basil for garnish

Instructions:

1. Olive oil is heated over medium heat in a large pot.
2. Cook the onion until it becomes clear.
3. Add the minced garlic and cook for another minute.
4. Stir in diced eggplant, zucchini, bell peppers, and dried spices.
5. Cook the vegetables for about 10 to 15 minutes or until soft.
6. Add diced tomatoes, stir, and cook for another 5 minutes.
7. Salt and pepper can be added to taste.
8. Serve the mixture of ratatouille over cooked brown rice.
9. Add chopped fresh basil to the top.

Nutrition (per serving):

- Calories: ~300
- Protein: ~6g
- Carbohydrates: ~50g
- Fiber: ~8g
- Fat: ~10g

THREE-BEAN AND BARLEY CHILI

Ingredients:

- 1/2 cup cooked barley
- 1/2 cup canned kidney beans, drained and rinsed
- 1/2 cup canned black beans, drained and rinsed
- 1/2 cup canned pinto beans, drained and rinsed
- 1 cup diced tomatoes
- 1 cup diced bell peppers (any colour)
- 1 cup diced onion
- 2 cloves garlic, minced
- 4 cups vegetable broth
- 2 teaspoons chilli powder
- 1 teaspoon ground cumin
- 1/2 teaspoon smoked paprika
- Salt and pepper to taste
- Olive oil for cooking
- Chopped fresh cilantro for garnish
- Greek yoghurt for serving (optional)

Instructions:

1. Olive oil is heated over medium heat in a big pot.
2. Add chopped bell peppers and onion. Cook the onion until it is clear.
3. Add the minced garlic and cook for another minute.
4. Mix in diced tomatoes, cooked barley, kidney beans, black beans, pinto beans, veggie broth, chilli powder, ground cumin, smoked paprika, salt, and pepper.
5. Bring the chilli to a boil, turn down the heat and let it cook for about 20 to 25 minutes.
6. Taste the food and, if necessary, change the spices.
7. You can put chopped fresh cilantro and a dollop of Greek yoghurt on top of the three-bean and barley soup.

Nutrition (per serving):

- Calories: ~300
- Protein: ~10g
- Carbohydrates: ~50g
- Fiber: ~12g
- Fat: ~4g

ROASTED RED PEPPER AND HUMMUS WRAP

Ingredients:

- 1 large whole wheat tortilla
- 1/4 cup hummus
- 1/4 cup roasted red pepper strips
- 1/4 cup baby spinach leaves
- 1/4 cup sliced cucumber
- 1/4 cup sliced red onion
- 1/4 cup crumbled feta cheese
- Olive oil for cooking

Instructions:

1. Put the whole wheat tortilla on a clean surface and spread it flat.
2. Spread hummus on the bread in an even layer.
3. Put red pepper strips, baby spinach leaves, cucumber slices, red onion slices, and chopped feta cheese on one half of the tortilla.
4. Fold the sides of the tortilla in, then tightly roll it up to make a wrap.

5. On medium heat, put the olive oil in a pan.
6. Cook the wrap for 2 to 3 minutes on each side until the tortilla is crisp and the filling is hot.
7. Cut the wrap with hummus and roasted red peppers in half and serve.

Nutrition (per wrap):

- Calories: ~300
- Protein: ~10g
- Carbohydrates: ~40g
- Fiber: ~8g
- Fat: ~12g

FIBER-PACKED MIXED BERRY CHIA JAM

Ingredients:

- 2 cups mixed berries (blueberries, strawberries, raspberries, etc.)
- Two tablespoons chia seeds
- 2 tablespoons honey or maple syrup
- 1 teaspoon lemon juice

Instructions:

1. Mix mixed berries and honey or maple syrup in a pot.
2. Heat over medium heat, stirring every so often, until the berries break down and their juices come out.
3. Use a fork or a potato masher to mash the berries to the desired consistency.
4. Add chia seeds and lemon juice and stir.

5. Keep cooking for 5–10 minutes or until the chia seeds make the mixture thicker.
6. Take the jam off the heat and let it cool.
7. Put the jam in a jar in the fridge until you're ready to use it.
8. The mixed berry chia jam is full of fibre so you can spread it on toast, yoghurt, or rice.

Nutrition (per tablespoon):

- Calories: ~20
- Carbohydrates: ~5g
- Fiber: ~2g
- Sugars: ~3g

THAI LENTIL AND VEGETABLE STIR-FRY

Ingredients:

- 1 cup cooked green or brown lentils
- 2 cups mixed vegetables (bell peppers, carrots, snap peas, etc.)
- 2 tablespoons low-sodium soy sauce
- 1 tablespoon hoisin sauce
- 1 tablespoon lime juice
- 1 tablespoon sesame oil
- 1 teaspoon grated ginger
- 2 cloves garlic, minced
- Crushed red pepper flakes to taste
- Chopped fresh cilantro for garnish

- Chopped peanuts for garnish (optional)

Instructions:

1. Heat sesame oil over medium-high heat in a wok or a big skillet.
2. Chop some garlic and grate some ginger. Cook for about a minute or until the smell is pleasant.
3. Add the mixed veggies and cook for a few minutes until they soften.
4. Stir in the cooked beans and cook for another 2–3 minutes.
5. Mix low-sodium soy sauce, hoisin sauce, lime juice, and a pinch of crushed red pepper flakes in a small bowl with a whisk.
6. Pour the sauce over the lentils and vegetables and stir to thoroughly cover them.
7. Cook for another two to three minutes or until everything is hot.
8. Take it off the heat and, if you want, top it with chopped fresh cilantro and chopped peanuts.
9. Serve the bean and vegetable stir-fry with brown rice or quinoa that has been cooked.

Nutrition (per serving):

- Calories: ~300
- Protein: ~12g
- Carbohydrates: ~45g
- Fiber: ~10g
- Fat: ~8g

CONCLUSION:

We hope you've learned a lot and had fun as we get to the end of the High Fiber Cookbook. Our cooking adventure has been about the fantastic world of high-fibre foods, how they can change your health, and how you feel about food. With each recipe, we tried to show that healthy food can be both good for you and incredibly tasty.

As you put this guide away, we want you to remember the lessons you've learned. Adopting a high-fiber diet isn't just a short-term choice; it's a permanent change that will bring long-term benefits. By making these fibre-rich meals a regular part of your life, you make a long-term health investment.

Remember that a high-fibre diet has benefits that go beyond the body. By giving your body meals full of nutrients, you also connect the food you eat and your general health. We hope this cookbook has made you want to try the many different items, play around with flavours, and make your high-fibre masterpieces.

This cookbook pushes you to take back your kitchen and your health at a time when convenience is often more important than nutrition. Every bite you eat is a chance to feed yourself, and by putting fibre-rich foods at the top of your list, you're choosing to live your best life.

As you keep working on your health, remember that the High Fiber Cookbook is more than just a collection of meals. It's a great example of how food can change people's lives and a good lesson that eating well can be fun and satisfying. We're happy to have been a part of your journey through the world of food, and we hope that the recipes you've found here will stay on your table for years to come.

Here's to good health, tasty food, and a future with many tasty options. Happy cooking and good health.

The End

Printed in Great Britain
by Amazon

27396161R00183